BUSINESS BASICS

A Guide to Who Does What
in Today's Organizations

BUSINESS BASICS

A Guide to Who Does What
in Today's Organizations

by

Mike Moyer and Jerry Fuller

Made possible through grants from

The James S. Kemper Foundation

ISBN:9780692495629

This publication is designed to provide accurate and authoritative information in regard to the subject matter covered. It is sold with the understanding that the publisher is not engaged in rendering legal, accounting, or other professional service. If legal advice or other expert assistance is required, the services of a competent professional person should be sought. —*From a Declaration of Principles Jointly Adopted by a Committee of the American Bar Association and a Committee of Publishers and Associations*

All brand names and product names used in this book are trademarks, registered trademarks, or trade names of their respective holders.

Published by the James S. Kemper Foundation
Chicago, IL
www.JSKemper.com

This book and online course are dedicated to the many bright students who are unfamiliar with the business world and have not yet decided on a career path. Our hope is that this information will help them understand how business organizations function and be successful in their internships and first jobs.

FOREWARD

In 1942, James S. Kemper established an independent, private foundation. Today the Kemper Foundation is committed to shaping well-rounded future business leaders, with a special focus on the insurance industry.

As part of this effort, we have created a successful internship program designed to help prepare undergraduate students for their careers.

We thought Business Basics would be a good way to further our mission by providing some practical advice for navigating a career path in business.

The components of the Business Basics program include not only this book, but an online course that can be found at **JSKemper.org.**

We hope that this book and the accompanying online course will help students prepare for, and get excited about, the wonderful opportunities in the world of business!

Sincerely,

Donald Southwell
Chairman, President and CEO
Kemper Corporation

TABLE OF CONTENTS

INTRODUCTION 1

THE ORGANIZATION 3

PEOPLE AND DEPARTMENTS................................. 11

FUNCTIONAL AREAS 35

MARKETING 45

SALES 69

OPERATIONS 75

PRODUCT PRODUCTION 81

HUMAN RESOURCES 97

FINANCE & ACCOUNTING 119

THE BUSINESS LIFECYCLE 139

CONCLUSION.. 155

ABOUT THE AUTHORS 159

INTRODUCTION

For-profit businesses and nonprofit organizations can be very complex. There are lots of people working at computers in cubicles sending emails, meeting in conference rooms and chit-chatting around the water cooler. To many people life in this environment is perfectly normal. However, if you are new to the scene it can be confusing and overwhelming. It's easy for business men and women to take the business environment for granted, so very few of them really stop and share the basics with the new generation of business employees.

This book provides a high-level overview of the basic functions of a business and the people responsible for planning and managing the activities of the business.

The purpose of this book is to help you become acclimated to the business environment as quickly as possible so you can navigate your own responsibilities within the firm with more confidence. We want to help you get started on the right foot with your job, and help you to leave a positive impression on your coworkers and supervisors.

Chapter 1

THE ORGANIZATION

While all organizations are unique, they share some basic commonalities that allow them to function in the economic and legal environments in which they exist. Companies are organized in a way to maximize their ability to deliver a quality product or service, and to minimize the overall cost of delivering the product or service. These two attributes are also known as effectiveness and efficiency. Both are concepts that are at times opposed to one another. For instance, you may be able to deliver a higher quality product, but the cost of doing so may exceed the customer's willingness to pay for it. An organization must continually optimize its operations to strike the right balance. And, of course, they must do it legally.

BUSINESS FUNCTIONS

All businesses are comprised of a fairly standard set of disciplines that allow them to operate. For instance, all businesses must have a financial component that is responsible for receiving money from customers, investors, and partners, and for distributing money to employees, suppliers, partners, and (hopefully) investors.

In some companies, like a small consulting business, many of the functions of a business are handled by one person. The consultant has to collect money from clients and pay rent and utilities, such as phone and internet access. No person can do everything, however, and anything they can't do themselves they will have to pay someone else to do for them. If a client needs a service the consultant can't provide, the consultant may have to sub-contract the job out to someone else.

In other companies, like a Fortune-500 corporation, there are many people who focus their time and attention on a single function within the business. There may be dozens or even hundreds of people who do nothing but pay bills, for instance. These businesses are more complex and require a hierarchy to manage all the activity. Even with this complexity, however, there are predictable structures that have evolved over time.

THE PURPOSE OF THE ORGANIZATION

There are two primary types of organizations. There are for-profit organizations and nonprofit organizations. Each type of organization has a different purpose that has an impact on how it operates.

All organizations have three basic types of people:

The first are the people who provide the money to fund the organization. In a for-profit business these people are called investors. In a nonprofit organization these people are called donors or benefactors.

The next type of people are those who do the work of the organization by creating and delivering value. In a for-profit business these are the employees. In a nonprofit organization they are often called volunteers (a paid volunteer is also called an employee).

The last group of people is those who receive the value created by the organization. For-profit businesses have customers; nonprofit organizations have beneficiaries.

While the activities of both types of organizations are similar, their purposes are quite different.

In a for-profit business the purpose is to create profits for the investors. So, at a basic level, the job of the employees is to get money out of the pockets of customers, and put it into the pockets of investors. To do this they have to efficiently produce something of value for customers so that customers will buy it for more than it costs the company to produce. The leftover money, also called "profit" is then distributed to investors or reinvested into the company.

Figure 1: The Purpose of the For-Profit Company

To make more profit, a company is constantly working to both increase sales of its products or services, and decrease the costs of producing its products or delivering its services.

Conversely, in a nonprofit business the purpose is to create benefits for beneficiaries. So, at a basic level the job of the volunteer is to get money out of the pockets of benefactors and put it into the pockets of beneficiaries. While most nonprofit organizations don't literally distribute cash to beneficiaries, they still have to maximize the value delivered to them so that benefactors will continue to support the mission of the organization with donations. A nonprofit's mission is supposed to be something dedicated to the greater public good.

Figure 2: The Purpose of the Nonprofit Organization

So, the fundamental difference between a for-profit business and a nonprofit organization is the flow of money through the organization. One flows towards investors, the other flows towards beneficiaries. In both cases, however, workers need to maximize the efficiency with which they operate.

The better the employees and volunteers are at being efficient, the higher their own personal rewards will be. Really effective leaders of for-profit or nonprofit organizations can earn millions in salary in bonuses because they are able to provide important benefits to lots of people who need them. As you develop your own career, keep in mind that being an effective employee is being someone who can maximize the "flow" in an organization.

CORPORATE STRUCTURE

The structures of a for-profit business and a nonprofit organization are similar, even though their purposes are different. The parts of the business that we will cover in this book include Marketing, Sales, Finance, Accounting, Human Resources, Research & Development, Operations and Customer Service. Just about every position within the firm can fit into one of these departments.

In this book we will provide enough detail on those structures so that you will be able to identify who does what in your organization, and you will understand how the overall hierarchy works and how it relates to an individual's responsibilities and authority. We will cover details of both for-profit and nonprofit organizations, with an emphasis on for-profit companies.

More importantly, by the end of this book you will have a solid understanding of how you and your work fit into the overall activities of the firm, and hopefully discover what parts of the organization you personally find most interesting.

All jobs are part of business organizations and there is a great place for everyone. We hope that through some basic business education and practical experience you will be able to begin charting your own future—a future that is perfect for you!

Chapter 2

PEOPLE AND DEPARTMENTS

Most successful companies are organized in a hierarchy that can be depicted by an organizational chart, or "org chart" for short. The org chart shows reporting relationships between different people in the organization. A reporting relationship refers to where an individual's immediate responsibilities lie. The person you "report to" in an organization is the person in charge of making sure that you understand what is expected of you, that you have the resources required to get your job done, and that you are getting your job done. Likewise, you have a responsibility to regularly communicate with that person to clarify his or her expectations and provide status updates with regard to your progress.

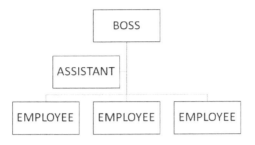

Figure 3: Organizational Chart

Reporting relationships also serve as the primary means of communication within an organization. If the senior management team outlines a new business strategy, your role with respect to that strategy is likely to be communicated to you through your immediate supervisor.

In large companies, an organizational chart can have many levels that create a pyramid. The few individuals with the most responsibility are at the highest level, and the individuals with the least responsibility are towards the bottom. Your level within the organization, therefore, will have a lot to do with how much you get paid, how much responsibility you have, and how much decision-making authority you have.

Two people in different functional departments may be at similar levels in the organization. It is likely that these people have a similar amount of responsibility and authority within the organization.

You may hear that a senior-level person must "approve" or "sign-off" on something before it can move forward. For instance, a manager in a factory might want to order a new piece of equipment. He may need approval from a higher-level manager if he does not have the authority to approve the expense himself. He might have the ability to approve expenses up to $500, but his manager may have the authority to approve expenses up to $5,000. If the equipment costs under $500 he won't need approval; if it costs over $500, but under $5,000 his manager could approve the expense. If it's over $5,000, his manager may have to present the equipment proposal to higher-level managers until one of them has enough authority to approve the expense.

This chain of command with regard to expenses helps the company control costs by empowering only select individuals to incur costs on behalf of the firm.

A person's authority is not limited to expenses, however. Managers may have to approve new product concepts before they can be produced, or approve new marketing messages before they are released to the public. The hierarchy ensures that decisions are made at the appropriate level in the organization.

The specific responsibilities of different roles in a company can vary from company to company, and there is often overlap between people's jobs. However, the following descriptions are good guidelines for who does what within an organization's hierarchy.

BOARD OF DIRECTORS

At the top of the pyramid you will often find the person who occupies the role of President or Chief Executive Officer (CEO). However, the ultimate decision-maker for important decisions is the Board of Directors (BOD). The Directors are "above" the senior management team and are the people who are responsible for making sure the organization is acting in a way that best serves the goals of the investors, in the case of a for-profit company, or the public, in the case of a nonprofit company.

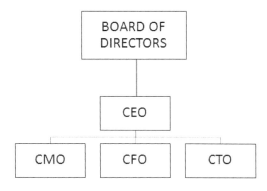

Figure 4: The Board of Directors is at the top of the Organizational Chart

A member of the Board of Directors is often referred to as being a "fiduciary." A fiduciary is someone who is expected by any moral, ethical or legal standard to act entirely within the best interests of the entity he or she represents.

In a for-profit company the Board of Directors has a fiduciary duty to the company's investors. The directors are often appointed or elected by the investors to make sure that their money is kept safe, and that the management team is making responsible decisions with regard to the money.

If a company is owned by a single person who also operates the company, there may not be a board of directors. If the individual invested her own money in the company she doesn't need anyone looking over her shoulder to determine the best way to spend the money. However, if other people—like banks, private investors, or venture capital companies - also invested in the company, they will expect to have representation on the board.

Boards of Directors often use voting to make big decisions about the company. Big decisions can include approving major expenses (like buying a new factory), managing the salaries of the senior-level staff, determining major changes in corporate strategy, and even deciding whether or not to sell the company or merge with another company. Because voting is important, boards usually have an odd number of members so there won't be ties.

Board members may represent different investors or groups of investors, usually in proportion to the amount of money invested. For instance, if a bank loans a company a substantial amount of money, it may require a board seat as a condition of the loan. This will allow the bank to keep a close eye on how the money is being spent and help steer the company in a direction that will enable it to be able to pay back the loan. An investment firm might invest money in the company and require a board seat as a condition of the investment. That board member's job will be to maximize the return on the investment. Both the board members have specific goals in mind for the people they represent, so board rooms are often places of heated debate.

In a publicly-traded company, board members are elected by the individual shareholders. If you personally own stock in a public company you may occasionally be asked to vote for board members. The more shares you own, the more votes you get, and the more you can influence who sits on the board. Individuals who own 51% of a company's stock can outvote anyone and, therefore, control the company.

In a nonprofit organization the board of directors has a fiduciary duty to the general public, but the directors may also be representatives of major benefactors. Many of them will be benefactors themselves. Their main goal is to make sure that the money being donated to the organization furthers the mission of the nonprofit organization as efficiently and effectively as possible.

In addition to their role as a fiduciary for the general public, nonprofit board members are often asked to help raise money for the organization and even donate themselves. Nonprofits with a lot of large donors may have a lot of board members!

CHAIRMAN OF THE BOARD

The Chairman of the Board is the board member who works most closely with the management team. The Chairman is elected by the other board members or shareholders.

The Chairman's primary job is to monitor the operations of the company and to make sure that big decisions get attention from the board. The Chairman is the person who sets the agenda for regular board meetings and assigns specific board members to dig deeper into specific areas of the business. For instance, a Chairman might want to form a compensation committee which would be made up of several board members who will research best practices for management compensation and report back to the board. This allows the board members to make sure all aspects of the business are getting the attention they deserve.

The Chairman of the Board has a great deal of power within an organization. The Chairman has significant influence on what decisions are made, how they are made and when they are made.

CHIEF EXECUTIVE OFFICER

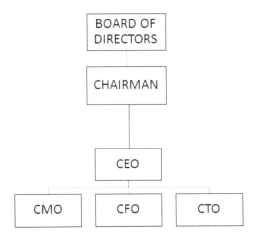

Figure 5: The Chairman works for the BOD and the CEO works for the Chairman (usually)

Unlike a member of the Board of Directors, who may have a part-time role in the company, a company's CEO usually has day-to-day responsibilities within the company. At the highest level, his or her job is to deploy the resources of the organization according to the intent of the Board of Directors. She or he also makes sure that the decisions made by the Board of Directors are communicated throughout the organization, and that they are addressed in a timely manner. CEOs generally have the highest level of authority within an organization. This means they can make big decisions and authorize big expenses. Limits on their authority are set by the Board of Directors. In good times the board may grant more authority to a CEO, in bad times they may tighten the reins a little.

The CEO is also the person who leads the organization into the future by setting a clear vision for the future and putting the organization on the path to realizing the vision. Steve Jobs was the quintessential CEO. He provided charisma and leadership to Apple. At the same time, Jobs followed the direction provided by his board to make sure the company provided a good return for investors. A powerful vision without some sound financial objectives can be a disaster.

PRESIDENT

The topmost manager in an organization, aside from the CEO, is the company's President. The President usually reports to the CEO and is responsible for execution. He or she develops a plan for achieving the vision of the CEO within the parameters set by the board of directors. The President makes sure the right people are part of the senior staff, and that they are all working towards a common understanding of what needs to be done. The President keeps a close eye on the progress people are making towards their goals, and helps implement reward and incentive programs for senior managers.

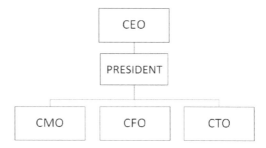

Figure 6: The Senior-Level Executives

If a department is struggling, the company President is responsible for figuring out what's wrong and taking steps to turn the department around. This can include retraining the staff, reorganizing the staff, or even replacing unproductive employees.

In nonprofit companies the President's title is often that of "Executive Director" instead of President.

In many companies the same person holds the title of both President and CEO implying that he or she is responsible for both setting the vision for the company and execution.

Titles and job descriptions always have a lot of overlap. What the President does in one company, the CEO may do in another. Few jobs, especially senior-level jobs, have "hard edges" on their responsibilities.

C-LEVEL MANAGERS

You will often hear about CTOs, CMOs, COOs and CFOs and other "C-Level" managers. The "C" stands for Chief, and represents the highest level of authority within a given department in an organization. The scope of their authority will vary based on the size and relative importance of their function. This group of managers is kind of like the President's "posse". They represent the primary functional areas of the company and provide management oversight for the daily activities of the department.

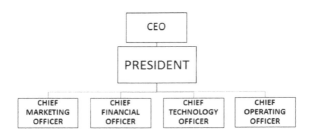

Figure 7: The C-Suite

Since C-level people are often called upon to provide ideas on how the company can best realize its vision, they may have a strategic as well as a management responsibility within the company.

It is quite common for C-Level managers to have deep experience in their functional areas and hold advanced degrees, such as an MBA, MS, or even a law degree. Investors give these people a lot of responsibility and they want to make sure they have the knowledge to make the right decisions. C-level titles include:

Chief Operating Officer - This person is responsible for how the company produces and delivers its products or services. The COO should have a keen eye for efficiency. The profits of a company are directly related to how efficiently the company operates. The COO often has the most authority of all the senior management staff.

In smaller companies it is not unusual for the President of the company to have a dual title. It is common for an individual, such as a founder, to have the title of President & CEO, for instance. However, as the company grows, founders typically stay in a visionary role and hire someone else to manage the daily activities of the firm. In these cases, a new President may be hired and given operating responsibility. The COO role is often coupled with the role of President in small and mid-size companies, and that person is called the President & COO.

COOs generally have good organizational and analytical skills with better attention to detail than a visionary CEO. Many entrepreneurs have a hard time managing the day-to-day operations of a company. They find the management tasks boring. However, for the right person, the role of COO is extremely exciting and rewarding.

COOs often have MBAs with concentrations in general management, strategy or operations.

Chief Marketing Officer - The CMO is in charge of connecting the company to the outside world by getting the product or service in front of people who are most likely to buy it. Marketing roles can be incredibly diverse so marketing professionals often have to master a very broad set of skills. A CMOs skills range from extremely creative to extremely analytical.

CMOs often have advanced degrees in marketing or management, but sometimes they have degrees in art and design.

Chief Financial Officer - Every organization has to be responsible for how it handles money. The more money an organization manages the more complicated this responsibility becomes. The CFO is the person who is in charge of making sure the money is flowing through the organization in the right direction. In a for-profit company the money should be flowing towards the investors. In a nonprofit company the money should be flowing towards the beneficiaries.

CFOs spend a lot of their time monitoring where the money is at any given time, and reporting back to the rest of the senior management team at regular intervals. Companies have many different kinds of reports, but the main reports are known as financial statements. These include the Balance Sheet, Income Statement, and Statement of Cash Flows.

The CFO also manages the people who are responsible for collecting money from customers, and paying money to vendors. The timing of these activities can have a profound effect on how well the company manages money. CFOs always want to collect money as quickly as possible and pay money as slowly as possible.

Lastly, the CFO helps manage the financial risk the company takes on as part of its operation. Many companies extend credit terms to customers instead of collecting up front. This enables them to get more customers because they make it easier for the customer to pay, so credit terms can be a good way to grow a business. However, there is always a risk that someone won't pay. The CFO keeps a close eye on who is paying and develops policies to establish the conditions under which the company will extend credit terms.

Other types of risk may pertain to the ways in which the company invests its excess cash. Rather than keeping cash in a savings account, the CFO might decide to invest some in the stock market for a higher return rate. This is more risky, but also provides a higher return. The CFO must make sure that he has enough money to run the business in the short term, while maximizing the return of money in the long term.

CFOs often have advanced degrees in finance, such as an MBA or MS. Many of them hold special financial certifications such as a Chartered Financial Analyst (CFA) or a Certified Public Accountant (CPA).

Chief Technology Officer - These days nearly every company has a technology component, and the CTO is the person who is responsible for making sure everything runs smoothly. These days the term "technology" is fairly broad, so a CTOs role can also be very broad. Some companies figure that anything that can be plugged into a network is technology. This includes all computers, servers, phone systems, and all the related hardware and software.

In some companies technology is the product. A software or internet company, for instance, has technology as its core offering. In these cases the CTO plays a strategic leadership role and helps the CEO shape the vision for the company.

In other cases technology is primarily a support function to the organization. In these cases the CTO manages information systems (like financial and manufacturing systems), and desktop support to employees for their PCs. In these cases it is less common to use the title CTO and more common to use the title Vice President of Technology.

CTOs often have degrees in engineering or computer science. Many of them start out as computer programmers or network specialists and work their way up. In large organizations they have to delegate programming and network support to their employees.

OTHER C-LEVEL TITLES

Whenever a job is granted the title of "Chief" it designates the role as having strategic importance to the organization. Because there are so many different types of companies, there are many functions within the organization that have C-level status. For instance, if the company relies heavily on information in order to run, they might have a Chief Information Officer (CIO) who is responsible for gathering and disseminating information throughout the organization.

A company that prides itself with customer service may have a Chief Relationship Officer who ensures that all employees understand how to treat customers.

There are companies that have Chief Happiness Officers who make sure that employees and customers are becoming happier as a result of their relationship with the firm.

If you are in an organization that has an unusual C-level position you can bet that the company places enormous value on that role, and that the individual is responsible for something core to the company's culture. It would be smart to set up some time with that person and learn more about the role.

BELOW C-LEVEL

A company's senior management team includes the CEO, the President, C-Level executives and other department heads. All people in the organization report to the CEO through this senior team. The titles each person in the company has indicates his or her level of responsibility and authority within the organization.

In many cases, especially in larger companies with more formal Human Resource Departments, titles indicate a compensation level as well. As a rule, the higher your title, the more money you make.

VICE PRESIDENTS

A Vice President usually overseas one or more related functional areas within the firm and helps develop and implement strategies that help to achieve the company's vision. VP's translate the direction of the senior management team into action plans. They are often the main conduit between the senior levels of an organization and the lower levels.

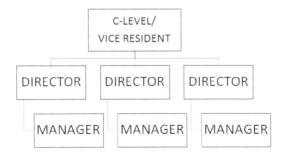

Figure 8: Vice Presidents, Directors and Managers

One of the main functions of a VP is to create the department's annual budget and manage the budget throughout the year. Budgeting is an important part of any company, and each VP is responsible for letting the senior team know what each department will need in order to function. Each departmental budget gets added into an overall operating budget that usually requires approval from the President, the CEO, and/or the Board of Directors.

Once a budget is approved, the VP will generally have the ability to authorize just about any expenses that the department incurs, with one major exception: personal expenses. When an individual at any level of the organization incurs personal expenses he or she must have them approved by his or her immediate supervisor. Personal expenses include travel expenses and other expenses incurred by the individual on behalf of the firm for which reimbursement is expected. If you incur expenses during your employment your supervisor will probably ask you to submit your receipts and an expense report to be approved.

VPs are also responsible for the performance of their departments, and for making key hiring and firing decisions within their functional areas.

Depending on the size of the organization and the seniority of the individual, the VP-level title might also be called an Executive Vice President (EVP) or a Senior Vice President (SVP). These titles recognize not only the functional role of the individual, but also their importance as a member of the strategic team. There are also Junior Vice Presidents (JVP) and Assistant Vice Presidents (AVP) which are usually stepping-stones towards the role of VP.

VP-level employees often have advanced-level degrees relevant to their functional areas. MBAs are quite common.

DIRECTORS

Not to be confused with a member of the Board of Directors, Director-level employees translate plans into action. Generally speaking, while senior-level managers (VP and above) are primarily concerned with planning and management, Director-level managers are in charge of getting stuff done in the organization. Director-level titles are often defined by the specific area of responsibility. For instance, the Director of Ecommerce would be directly responsible for operating an ecommerce site. The

Director of Direct Mail would be directly responsible for executing direct mail programs based on direction from the Vice President.

In most large organizations, Director-level jobs are middle-management positions, and many of them are stepping-stones to greater responsibility, such as that of a VP-level position. You will also hear of promotions to Junior Director or Senior Director, which are ways of recognizing an individual's contribution to the firm with small increases in responsibility.

MANAGERS

Manager-level positions usually imply that an individual has management responsibility for a team of task-specific employees. A manager is someone who has demonstrated an ability to understand how to do a specific task and to train others to do it as well. The manager is often in charge of hiring team members or firing those who are unproductive. The Manager of Accounts Payable, for instance, would manage a team of administrative employees who process payments to a company's partners and vendors. A Sales Manager usually manages a team of salespeople and is responsible for their performance.

Generally speaking, Managers are the lowest level of management in an organization. Some of them can be quite well paid and many people find that they enjoy working at this level with little interest in moving up the ladder.

OTHER TITLES

Below Manager there are all sorts of different titles that help us better understand the functional role of the individual. Entry-level jobs are often designated as "Coordinator" or "Associate" positions. For instance, an entry-level job in an ad agency is often called an Account Coordinator and an entry-level job in an accounting department might be an Accounts Payable Associate. These are titles for people who don't have management responsibilities, just functional responsibilities. In other words, their main job is to do something, not to manage someone doing something. A Field Service Technician provides technical service in the field, he doesn't manage others. His manager would be the Field Service Manager.

If the individual's job is to help another person do her job that individual is often referred to as an Assistant. An Executive Assistant, for instance, provides support services to a senior-level executive. He might sort the Executive's mail, take phone calls, or help organize travel arrangements.

These titles are the first rung in a ladder that leads all the way up to the Chairman of the Board.

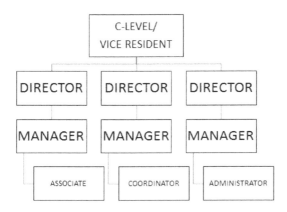

Figure 9: Other titles

Titles help us to know who does what, how much authority each person has, and what kind of responsibility each has. There are lots of different titles and not every title will follow exactly the outline we have covered. If you find someone called Manager who doesn't manage anyone, don't worry about it.

Titles help organizations stay organized. You might hear of a company that "doesn't do titles." These kind of unstructured environments work well for small companies and startups, but you will rarely find a formidable company that doesn't benefit from organizational structure.

Chapter 3

FUNCTIONAL AREAS

Companies are made up of different departments that are responsible for different activities within the firm. In smaller companies certain individuals will wear many hats and perform many functions. In larger companies the departments are more narrowly focused. Both situations have their own challenges and benefits. Communication across functional areas is rarely a problem in small companies but often a problem in larger companies. Functional expertise is often a problem in small companies but less of a problem in large companies.

Companies depend a lot on different processes to operate. The larger the company, the more processes it has and the more complex it becomes. In large companies processes can be very formal and well-defined. In small companies they may be more informal with people doing things their own ways.

For instance, in a small restaurant the chef might prepare a hamburger based on his or her previous experience making hamburgers. This is fine if there is only one restaurant, but if you have more than one and every cook is making hamburgers his or her own way you will have inconsistent quality. In a national fast-food restaurant the process for making a hamburger is a well-documented procedure with very specific requirements. The individual cooks may not like the inability to be creative, but the company has to be able to manage the consistency of the product if they are to grow.

In order for a company to grow they must build the right processes and put the right people in place to execute. Similar processes can be grouped into departments. The processes for paying bills, reimbursing employees, and sending out invoices all deal with the banking functions of an organization, and therefore are logically grouped into the accounting department.

Similarly the processes for searching for employees, hiring employees, and administering employee benefits, all deal with employee functions of a company, and therefore are logically grouped into the human resource department.

Grouping processes and tasks into departments allows organizations to dedicate experienced employees to those areas where they can best execute.

Different companies have different operational designs, but most will have similar departments. The ways in which companies think about functions can be different from one to another as well. Some companies think marketing is primarily a sales-support function, while other companies see sales as part of the overall marketing function. The relative importance of the various functions within an organization can be understood by looking at the senior-level staff. If there is no senior-level marketing person in the company, it is likely that the company does not see marketing as an important function.

The structure of an organization reflects what the organization values. Companies that value technology will have senior-level technology professionals and those people will have a lot of power within the organization.

A company's values can have a profound effect on its success. While we will go into more depth on the different functional areas here is a high-level overview of the functional areas of an organization that we will cover:

MARKETING

The marketing department can have a very broad definition, but its main function is the design and promotion of a company's products and services. Research and Development, or R & D, is often part of marketing. The marketing staff can include people who are highly creative like designers and copywriters, as well as those who are highly analytical like database engineers.

SALES

The sales department is usually a very focused department whose primary responsibility is generating revenue for the firm. There are two primary types of sales teams. Inside sales are people who handle sales tasks from inside the office, and outside sales are people who travel to visit customers at the customers' sites. Good companies pay their sales team very well to keep them motivated to generate high revenues. Many salespeople are paid on commission, meaning they get a percentage of the revenue they generate.

CUSTOMER SERVICE

If it's the sales department's job to sell something to a customer, it's the job of customer service to keep it sold. Unhappy customers may ask for their money back or take their business somewhere else, so a company needs to do what it can to ensure that customers are happy with their purchases. The customer service department provides support for customers who have already purchased the product or service.

FINANCE

The finance department concerns itself with the business as an investment. They manage the company's money, secure debt and lines of credit, work with investors, prepare financial statements, and, if the company is publicly-traded, they monitor the stock and make sure that the company is compliant with SEC rules.

ACCOUNTING

Often confused with finance, the accounting department deals with the flow of money coming into and going out of an organization, and the ways in which each dollar is categorized so that the company can produce meaningful reports and pay the appropriate taxes. Companies, like people, pay all sorts of taxes. Income tax, sales tax, payroll tax and excise tax on certain items. Accounting professionals are usually very detail-oriented and have a vast knowledge of the rules and regulations for taxes and reporting requirements.

HUMAN RESOURCES

The department that handles all the hiring, development, assessment, advancement, and benefits programs of and for the employees of the company is called human resources. The main responsibility of a human resources department is to ensure that the organization has the right people with the right tools in the right jobs at the right time to help the company accomplish its goals.

OPERATIONS

All companies produce a product or service. The operations department is the group of people who produce them. In the case of a product company, the operations department manages factories, distribution centers, and transportation. In a service company, the operations department manages appointments and makes sure the services are being provided in a way that is consistent with the company's standards.

INFORMATION TECHNOLOGY

The information technology (IT) department is responsible for the design, implementation, and maintenance of information systems like phones, computers, tablets, data servers, and anything else that stores or transfers data. These data systems are critical to a company's ability to operate efficiently because they streamline the processes of the business. Reporting, for instance, is a critical process for the accounting department. In the old days accountants had to summarize accounting entries by hand. Today they can simply run a report from the accounting system. So, the process has been streamlined through information technology. What once might have taken weeks now takes only a few minutes. A good IT department will keep an eye out for opportunities like this and implement technology that helps people to become more efficient.

OTHER DEPARTMENTS

Companies may have other departments. If you see a department you don't recognize, simply follow the reporting relationship up to the CEO and you will better understand the primary function of the department and its relative importance. A manufacturing company that places high value on patents will often have a legal department that is part of the operations or product development group. For the most part, however, companies will have some mix of the above departments. In smaller companies people may wear many hats, but the above functions must be addressed in order for the company to operate properly.

HOW DEPARTMENTS WORK TOGETHER

Just as departments have their own internal processes, there are processes within companies that manage how departments work together. In small companies these processes are more informal. A person in sales might send an email to the IT department asking for some help with a computer issue. However, in larger companies that same process probably wouldn't work because it would be too hard to manage. The sales person in a large company might need to enter his problem in a support desk application and wait for a response. This process helps the IT department operate more efficiently and better understand the types of issues people are having. It might be easier just to send an email, but it would be less efficient in the long run.

As a rule, functional departments are the "go-to people" for their areas of responsibility. Whenever a department needs to hire someone, for instance, they would engage the help of the Human Resource department.

In some companies, departments will bypass people in a different department. A marketing VP may bypass the legal department and hire her own lawyer. The marketing VP may think that the internal legal process is too much trouble. When this happens communication breaks down and problems occur within the company. If the problem is big enough it will get the attention of senior management. Really large communication problems, which can be quite common, will get the attention of the Board of Directors.

When one department's processes create barriers for other departments, communication breaks down. Therefore, a department must constantly re-evaluate and redesign its processes to make them faster, easier and cheaper.

For instance, if outside salespeople have to ship their laptops to the IT department for service, the sales people might try to avoid the burden by trying to fix problems themselves, or by taking them to a local computer shop which may cause even more problems. In this case the process is too complicated. So, the IT department might decide to invest in remote desktop assistance for its outside sales team.

Small companies benefit from easy communication, informal processes, and quick response times. Many people like to work for small companies because they don't like the bureaucracy and formality of larger companies. However, without formal processes a company will have a hard time growing. The right processes allow companies to grow larger and larger. They lose some of the freedom of a small company, but can gain more in profits.

Companies that are growing are constantly improving their processes. This makes many people uncomfortable because they can be resistant to change. If you recognize change as an important part of how companies grow, and embrace or invent new ways of doing things, you will do well, get promoted, make more money, and enjoy your work. If you resist change you will stay at lower levels of the organization, get passed up for promotions, and find work frustrating.

Pay attention to the different processes within your company, and, before you suggest any changes, master the process and make sure you understand why it exists. Remember that the processes a company uses allow it to operate and grow and strike a balance between effectiveness and efficiency.

Chapter 4

MARKETING

The marketing department can have very diverse activities—ranging from the creative design of brand elements to technical analysis of customer data. One day the marketing team might be planning a trade show, and the next they might be visiting stores to take notes on competitive pricing, and the next day they might be conducting a focus group to learn more about what customers want in a new product, and the next day they might be conducting a sale seminar for the sales force.

Because the activities of the marketing department can be so diverse, higher-level managers must be not only creative and analytical, but also they must be able to deal with a high level of ambiguity. Lower-level employees tend to have more specific job descriptions. Marketing departments might have graphic designers or data analysts, for instance.

In small companies there may only be a few marketing people who handle lots of different things, while larger companies may have large departments with lots of specialists. In most cases the CEO, President, and other senior managers are closely involved in the marketing process.

THE FOUR P's

Marketing departments traditionally focus on the "Four P's" which are Product, Price, Place, and Promotion. This means their job is to define the product or service, figure out how much to charge for it, decide where the product will be sold, and execute programs—like advertising - to communicate the benefits of the product or service to existing and potential customers.

PRODUCT

It is the job of marketing to determine what products or services the company will offer. For a company that makes fishing tackle boxes, the marketing department will research the needs of fishermen, research the competitive products in the market, and design products they think fisherman will want to buy. If the company provides dry cleaning services the marketing department will research fashion trends and the types of materials that are most popular so they can design ways to keep them clean. When polyester became popular in the 1970's, dry cleaning companies had to learn to work with the new materials.

PRICING

How much a company charges for something is a very important issue that requires knowledge of the market and a keen understanding of how much it costs to create a product or deliver a service. Price something too high and people may not buy it, price it too low and the company may not make any money. The marketing department sets the price for the products or services the company sells.

PLACE

In order for someone to buy a product or service it must be made readily available. The place or method by which the product is made available, therefore, is extremely important. The marketing department often develops the channel strategy, which describes how customers and potential customers can learn about and acquire products.

Some products are only available on the internet. So, the internet is the place that the market department has deemed most valuable. For other products, like a can of soda, selling online might not be practical. So the place might include retail shops, restaurants, and vending machines.

The key to choosing the right place is to focus on maximizing profits by choosing an efficient channel. Selling soda through the internet would be time consuming and expensive, so even if the company were able to find online customers it might lose money. Selling through a soda fountain at a fast food restaurant, on the other hand, is quick and cheap, making it among the most profitable products available for sale.

PROMOTION

In order for people to want to buy something, they must find out that it exists in the first place. The marketing department is in charge of promoting a product or service to potential buyers. In some cases people tell each other about the product. This is known as "word-of-mouth" marketing, and it is an important part of promoting the product. It starts with a great product or service. Without word-of-mouth marketing a company will have a hard time growing.

Marketing departments supplement and accelerate word-of-mouth marketing through all sorts of marketing communication activities, including advertising, direct mail, email, and public relations.

THE FOUR C's

The Four P's are universally accepted as the main areas of focus for a marketing department. However, you may also hear about the "Four C's", which is a more modern interpretation of the marketing department's function that takes into account a more customer-focused agenda.

The Four C's stand for Consumer, Cost, Communication, and Convenience. The terms parallel the Four P's but provide a customer-focused spin. Some people feel the marketing department should worry less about the product and more about the needs of the consumer. Likewise, price is only one component of the overall cost to the consumer. For example, if the product is complicated, the consumer might spend time learning how to use it in addition to spending money to buy it, so time becomes part of the cost. Additionally, there may be ongoing maintenance fees that are not reflected in a simple pricing model.

The Four C's model replaces promotion with communication to reflect the importance of a two-way dialog with consumers. Lastly, the Four C's emphasize convenience rather than place, to remind marketers make it as easy as possible for a consumer to access the product. Take the example of selling soda online. In some cases buying online is so convenient that consumers are willing to pay the extra costs associated with shipping cans.

The Four P's and the Four C's are two different ways of looking at the same set of problems. They represent differences in attitude and mindset. In business, the language used can powerfully impact success. Successful companies care deeply about the words they use and how they are perceived by the outside word. These kinds of decisions are at the core of what the marketing department does.

The company you work for may have an entirely different way of thinking about the world. This is okay as long as they are covering the basics found in the Four P's or Four C's model.

Business to Business (B2B) companies, are companies that primarily provide products and services to other businesses. In contrast, Business to Consumer (B2C) companies, are companies that primarily provide products and services to consumers. In some cases a company will do both. For instance, a candy company will sell candy to candy stores, but may also use marketing to create demand among candy eaters. How a company accesses the market is known as a channel. Another candy company may bypass retailers and sell directly to candy eaters (also known as end-users), through a catalog or web site.

The markets the company targets will have a significant impact on the marketing tactics they choose to implement, and the channels they choose to work with. A candy company that sells to retailers may maintain a sales staff that calls on shop owners. In most cases it would be impractical for a sales person to call on an end-user. The candy end-user may only spend a few dollars on a candy bar once in a while, but the retailer could order thousands of dollars per year to stock his shelves.

Some marketing tactics, such as a direct sales force, are better suited for a B2B company. Others, like Super Bowl commercials, are perhaps better suited for a B2C company. Remember, companies have to trade off between effective and efficient. A salesperson may be more effective for selling to someone, but the cost may be too high. Conversely, a newspaper ad may be less effective than a salesperson, but it's a cheap way to get the message out. The effectiveness of an ad can be improved by testing messages and choosing the one that generates the most sales.

In your company it should be obvious which strategy, B2B or B2C, is used. If not, be sure to find out, since it will help you to better understand how the company works.

The Chief Marketing Officer (CMO) is the highest level marketing person in a company. He or she usually reports directly to the CEO or President, and sometimes has a Vice President-level title.

Under the Vice President are marketing directors that usually have a more specific focus, such as the Director of Online Marketing, the Director of Market Research, the Creative Director, or any one of many other Director-level titles. The Director-level person is responsible for implementing the strategy designed by the more senior-level staff members.

Below the Director level are managers who manage teams of people that focus on a set of discreet tasks. A Product Manager, for instance, manages the team of people who focus their attention on a single product or product line.

Within the marketing department are separate teams of people who focus on different tasks and processes. The marketing department is often divided up into smaller departments or teams. As mentioned before, similar processes are grouped so that people with expertise can focus on them. Graphic designers, for instance, have a process for gathering requirements from people, creating designs, gathering feedback, and capturing approvals from all the right managers.

PRODUCT DEVELOPMENT

The product development group, also known as Research and Development (R&D), has a systematic way of designing new products and services for customers. R&D isn't always in the marketing department, but the marketing department is a logical place for it. People in this group sometimes have engineering backgrounds with the talent to design software or products or services or whatever the company creates. Sometimes they have specialized educations in product development, industrial design, or a specialized craft.

In a wine company, the product development group, often led by the head winemaker, work in a laboratory where they test different blends of juice from different grapes, and experiment with fermentation times and techniques. In a vacuum cleaner company, the product development team probably consists of mechanical engineers who work with Computer Assisted Design (CAD) programs. In a law firm, the product development team might research new areas of law in which the firm can develop new practice areas.

Larger companies have formal processes that are well documented. The Product Development Process usually consists of stages that require management sign-off before the product can move to the next stage. Stage one usually consists of information gathering activities and requirements definition. During this stage the team outlines what the new product will do, who will use it, and financial projections on costs, sales and profits. The company's process will determine whose approval is necessary. In some companies, mid-level management approval is okay, but in others, the CEO, or even the Board of Directors, might have to review it. Different stages might require different levels of approval. Remember, approval processes help ensure that important issues or large expenses get the attention they deserve.

Other stages might include product design, customer research, prototype creation, field testing, manufacture design, vendor selection, and a host of other steps that take a product from idea to reality. At each stage the company must decide if the project is meeting its goals. If not, the company might cancel the new product and focus on something else. This is called a "stage-gate" process and it helps ensure that only viable concepts receive investments. Most new products never see the light of day!

RESEARCH

Marketing departments need a lot of research to ensure that they understand the needs of the customer. The research team is responsible for studying the market and bringing back information about the market that will help people do their jobs. There are two kinds of research. Secondary research is research gleaned from existing sources like the internet, newspapers, or pre-existing reports. Primary research includes focus groups, survey research, in-depth interviews with customers, and usability testing. Secondary research is cheaper and faster than primary research, but it may not be specific enough to answer the questions the firm needs to be answered.

Only very large companies maintain their own research teams; smaller companies usually outsource research to specialized firms that conduct research on the company's behalf.

MARKETING COMMUNICATION

The Marketing Communication (Mar-Com) team spends time figuring out how they are going to communicate the products and services to the world in a way that is consistent with the company's brand image. The better they do their job, the more word-of-mouth marketing they will generate.

The Mar-Com team can consist of graphic designers, copywriters, media buyers who buy ad space, print production experts, brand experts, and analysts who track the effectiveness of marketing campaigns. They design web sites, magazine ads, television commercials, sales materials, trade show promotions, investor relations materials, and anything else people need to communicate the features and benefits of their offerings to the world.

Branding

A company's brand determines how it is perceived by the outside world. Successful brands influence everything a company does, and provide the standards by which it makes decisions. And, while strong brands permeate every level and every department in a company, the Mar-Com team is often responsible for maintaining the company's brand.

Consumers who come in contact with strong brands understand what the brand stands for and what their experience will likely be like if they use the products or services of the company. For instance, if you were to see a product made by Apple you would instantly understand what kind of product it would be. Apple is an extremely powerful and important brand. Everyone at Apple lives the brand every day and the Mar-Com group is dedicated to making sure that all communication is telling the same story. They even go so far as to design a special staircase for their stores that is in line with the Apple brand.

Most people think that brands boil down to a logo and some ads. Weak brand companies think that brands are mere window-dressing and don't take branding seriously. Brands are much deeper than creative design or advertising gimmicks; they define everything about a company. A good brand is like a club that has its own style, customs, traditions and even language. Red Bull, for example, has created a culture with a focus on extreme sports, and they use weird words like "Flutag".

If you work for a company with a strong brand, it will be apparent and it will influence how you are expected to behave and make decisions. If you work for a company without a strong brand it will be less obvious how you are supposed to behave and make decisions beyond typical social norms. If you find yourself in this situation, don't worry, most companies haven't completely nailed their brand and most companies haven't created brands as powerful as Apple or Red Bull.

Public Relations

The Public Relations (PR) team is responsible for working with the media to tell the company's story and get the word out about what the company is doing. Journalists for TV, newspaper, magazine and online publications like to write stories about companies that they think their readers will find interesting. Keeping a company and a brand interesting isn't always easy, but good PR groups can find ways of generating interest. I mentioned Red Bull earlier. The main reason that Red Bull promotes extreme sports is because it gets the company a lot of attention from the media. There is only so much you can write about an energy drink, but there is a lot you can write about sports!

Public Relations is sometimes referred to as "unpaid media," meaning that the company does not pay for the publicity they receive. When a reporter writes a story about a company, she does not expect to get paid. In fact, if she did get paid she would be crossing an ethical line that would discredit the publication she writes for. Because PR is unpaid, it is more difficult to predict, and more difficult to plan. However, a good news story can do far more for a company than an ad.

Remember that generating word-of-mouth marketing is critical for a company's success. A good news story can be much more effective and much less expensive than a paid advertisement. People are much more likely to pass along a good story than they are an advertisement.

Advertising

Unlike PR, Advertising is known as "paid media," meaning that the company creates an ad and pays the publication to publish the ad. There are all sorts of advertising opportunities including TV, newspaper, magazines, billboards, online ads, and a variety of sponsorships. Sponsorships could range from something small like a local little league team to a NASCAR team. Sponsorships are also handled by the PR team, but when there is a paid media placement the advertising team usually gets involved.

The advertising team is also part of the marketing department. It consists of copywriters who write the headlines and the content for ads, designers who create the ads, media buyers who buy the placements for the ads, and account managers who keep everything organized. You may also find analysts and market researchers who find out what people want and analyze the results of ads so they can report back to the senior managers.

Online Advertising

Online advertising or online marketing is a specialized area of advertising that deals with the creation and placement of ads on the internet. There are a variety of ways to do this, but the most popular is called Pay Per Click (PPC) advertising where an advertiser will pay the publisher of a site only when an ad is clicked on. A site publisher is the person or company that owns the web site and creates the content on it. The ads you see on Facebook, Google and other search engines are most likely PPC ads. You will sometimes see PPC ads on other sites, especially news sites and blogs.

Advertisers pay anywhere from a few cents to over $50 each time a person clicks on their ad.

Figure 10: Google ads

As you might expect, the costs can add up quickly. When a person clicks on an ad, he is taken to a page on the advertiser site. This can be the homepage of the company, but better marketers use special landing pages that have specific offers for the visitor based on which ad is clicked. If someone clicks on a muffin ad, for instance, it would be better to take the person to a page about muffins, perhaps with a special muffin offer, rather than the bakery's home page. Really good marketers test different landing pages to see which page "converts" the best. A conversion means someone clicked on the ad and then took the desired action, such as filling out a form or ordering a product. If you are paying $50 each time someone clicks on an ad you better be good at creating pages on your site that turn visitors into buyers!

Cost Per Action (CPA) is another popular form of advertising where advertisers pay not on the click, but on the action the visitor takes upon reaching their site. When a purchase is the action, the advertiser often pays a commission to the owner of the site where the ad was placed. This is known as an affiliate program. Many people make a great living as affiliates, providing advertising to companies that pay commissions on sales.

In addition to being creative, good online advertising programs are highly analytical. Media companies usually provide detailed reporting on the origin of each and every click, the time of day, the number of times the ad was shown, and a plethora of other information that can help the advertiser home in on the most effective and efficient use of advertising dollars.

Search Engine Optimization

You may also hear the Online Marketing team refer to Search Engine Optimization (SEO). SEO is the practice of getting a web site to rank high on search engines when someone searches for a given search term or phrase. This is called *natural search*.

It's the search engine's best guess of what you are looking for. Results are based on a variety of attributes ranging from how relevant the content of your site is to how many other sites reference your site in their own content. How search engines rank sites is not only complicated, but also a moving target. Search engines are constantly tweaking their algorithms to improve results.

Trying to get a site to appear on the first page of a popular search term can be a lot of work. It requires some programming skills, writing skills, and relationship skills.

Direct Marketing

The Marketing department may also do Direct Marketing, which is most commonly in the form of direct mail or email. The Online Advertising team may also handle email marketing, but sometimes email is handled by the same people who handle the direct mail. There is often overlap between departments.

Direct Marketing is usually data intensive. In order to get the best response rate to a direct mail piece the marketer has to make sure they have a good mailing list of prospects that are likely to buy. The more information a marketer has on an individual the better. Basic direct mail programs consist of a mailing piece and a rented list of names or an internal list known as a house list. However, sophisticated direct marketers have lots of historical purchase data on individuals and can customize a message on each piece of mail.

A core feature of Direct Marketing is the ability to track the results of a campaign. All good direct mail pieces include a call to action, which is essentially a plea from the advertiser for the recipient to do something, such as sending in a response card or ordering the product. The number of people who respond divided by the number of people who received the solicitation is called the response rate. The response rate is an important measure of how effective the campaign was, and it is carefully tracked by marketers.

RESPONSE RATE = RESPONSES ÷ RECIPIENTS

Because direct mail is so easy to track, it is an ideal tool for running experiments. Marketers design tests to see which lists, offers, and creative executions get the best return on investment. It is not uncommon for response rates to double or even triple as a result of simple differences between mail pieces, such as using a different photo or headline.

When testing direct mail programs savvy marketers are careful to only test one variable, or one at a time. If they change too many variables at once, it will be impossible to tell which variable was responsible for the increase in response. This kind of testing is sometimes referred to as A/B testing.

If you are someone who likes to be creative, analytical and experimental you may like Direct Marketing.

In B2B companies, the marketing department often plays a critical role in generating sales leads. A sales lead usually comes in the form of the name and contact information of a person who may be interested in buying from the company. In addition to basic contact information, sales people like to have more details like company name, title, purchasing power, information about budgets, purchase time frame, and other data that will help the sales person better understand the needs of the customer. The more specific the lead is, the easier it is for the sales team to act on it. For a sales team, leads are everything. Such detailed information can be hard to come by, but good marketers will figure out a way.

Leads are important when the product or service is elaborate and requires a trained salesperson. Construction companies aren't likely to buy a crane through a magazine ad or web site. In most cases they are going to want to talk to a crane specialist who can help the company choose the best options based on their specific needs.

While most marketing tactics discussed above can be used for lead generation, there are some efforts that are better suited for B2B leads than others. Trade Shows are one example.

Trade Shows

Trade shows, sometimes called conferences, are gatherings of industry professionals usually at a hotel or conference center. There are shows that cater directly to consumers, but most shows are intended for a professional audience. They are usually organized by industry associations. For instance, the International Housewares Association organizes the Housewares trade show. People who buy and sell household items like plates, water filters, and vacuum cleaners visit the show from all over the world.

The typical trade show has three parts. The first is a series of educational classes, known as sessions, where professionals can learn about their industry or the skills they may need to do their job. The next part is the exhibit hall where vendors and service providers set up booths that display information about their company, products, and services. In some cases the booth can be nothing more than a table and some chairs, in other cases booths can represent millions of dollars in investment. The last part of the trade show is the entertainment. In an attempt to woo customers and prospects, companies will throw parties, have dinners, and take clients out for drinks. It is for this reason that many people really look forward to trade shows!

The marketing department works to help their company participate in all parts of the trade show. They will organize sessions taught by their management team, they will order the booth and provide people to work the booth by answering questions and demonstrate products, and they will plan customer appreciation and prospecting events.

Trade shows are big, expensive events and are a lot of work to pull off, but through them a good marketing team can generate dozens of great leads for their sales team.

Chapter 5

SALES

The sales department is often separate from the marketing department. Some companies are sales-driven, meaning they see the sales force as the main conduit to the customers and the outside word. Sales is "king" and the marketing department primarily exists to support sales efforts. In companies like this the marketing people spend a lot of time creating brochures, PowerPoint presentations, and other sales tools.

Other companies place more importance on the marketing function and value their brand over the sales function. In these companies marketing sets the stage for how sales operates by defining the sales program, messaging, process, and even the goals.

Either way, the sales department is often one of the most focused departments in the organization. Where the marketing department has many responsibilities the sales department generally has one: generating revenue.

Nothing is more important to a company than revenue. Without revenue there is no company. Investors and banks aren't willing to fund a company without revenue for very long, so unless a company can sell its products or services it won't be around very long.

Salespeople usually earn a small base salary along with a commission on the sales they generate. The percentage they earn varies, but is generally between 5% and 25% depending on their ability to hit sales goals. Good salespeople can be among the highest paid employees in the company and they should be. Without sales nobody has a job!

The sales department, like all departments, has its own processes. The sales process is what they use to turn a lead into a sale. A well-defined sales process includes sales stages, such the initial call to a prospect, needs analysis, value proposition, proposal delivery, and final sale. Leads go in one end of the process and some of them turn into sales.

SALE

Figure 11: The Sales Funnel

This is also known as the sales funnel. Few things are more important to a sales department than understanding its sales funnel. In some cases improving sales is as simple as generating more leads to put into the funnel. In other cases the team needs better training on how to handle each stage. For instance, they may need a new script for the initial call that will help them better communicate the product's benefits to the prospect.

Because sales are so important to all organizations there is often a lot of heated debate on the best way to do things. Sales people often blame the marketing department for poor sales. They might complain that there aren't enough leads, or that the product isn't right, or that the brochures need to be improved, or that the price is too high. Marketing, on the other hand, might complain that the sales team isn't aggressive enough, or won't follow the sales program, or doesn't appreciate the materials that were provided. It can be a constant struggle.

If you want to grow with your organization you will need to recognize that in order for the company to succeed all departments need to cooperate in ways that are productive. Constant improvement of each department's processes will make things work more smoothly, and provide more information about the root of problems.

Many sales teams use Customer Relationship Management (CRM) programs to help them manage their activities on a daily basis. These tools capture lead data from the marketing group and help the sales person manage all communication with them throughout the sales process. The marketing department can get reports from this system and identify areas where they can help support the sales department. The technology allows them to better manage the process and improve things that need attention.

If you like meeting new people and helping them solve their problems you might like to work in sales. Sales people often work very independently and may even work from home. Outside sales people who call on customers usually travel extensively. Many fly all over the country and the world to meet with customers. These days, however, online meeting spaces reduce the need for face-to-face meetings. Still, many salespeople will attest that there is no better way to build a relationship with someone than through an in-person meeting.

PARTNERSHIPS

All companies need partners to help them do things they can't do on their own. Marketing departments might rely on consultants for market research or advertising agencies to create ads and buy media. Often times a marketing department will hire freelance designers when full-time employees aren't required.

Some companies work with manufacturer representatives who work independently to sell products from a number of companies. They get paid a percent of the revenue they generate for the company. This is a great way for smaller companies to reach a larger audience without having to manage a sales staff.

Sales and Marketing are essential functions within an organization. Without them the company could not grow because there would be nobody around to create and promote products, and nobody around to sell them to customers.

Chapter 6

OPERATIONS

Where the sales and marketing teams focus heavily on generating revenues, the operations department focuses heavily on profitability. If the company can make and deliver the product or provide the service for less than they charge for it the company can generate profits.

Operations people spend a lot of their time reviewing data and fixing problems they find with the many processes within their company. They have to pay attention to detailed reports so they can understand how their processes are working. Operations people have a lot of reports and measures and indicators.

Think about operating a car. You have to keep tabs on many different things using the various gauges and indicators on the dash. You monitor the gas, the speed, the engine temperature, and other things that tell you how well the car is operating. You also rely on how the car feels when you are driving it. If the car doesn't feel right you have to pull over and check things under the hood. Sometimes warning lights come on and you will have to call in specialists. All of these things are similar to what a person in the operations department does for a company. Every part of the company is moving along and the job of operations people is to make sure it is all running smoothly.

When things aren't working properly they have to change things and tweak things. To continue the car analogy, perhaps it is something simple like changing the oil, or maybe it's something more complex like an engine overhaul. Perhaps the car is maxed out and the operations team recommends buying a new car altogether.

Sometimes seemingly simple changes in an operational process can have profound impact on productivity. Most people are familiar with an assembly line. In an assembly line, workers are each trained to perform a specific task. When they complete their task they pass the product to the next person. The assembly line is a very efficient and effective way to build products. However, there are times when workers are standing idle because the person in front of them hasn't completed his or her task. A manager who observes this may have to move people around the line, or do more training to increase productivity. While tweaking the steps in an assembly line and moving around workers can help increase the speed at which they build products, the impact is usually incremental. However in some cases a dramatic increase in productivity can be achieved by using a simple change called a bucket brigade.

In a bucket brigade assembly line, each worker learns his own task as well as the task of the person before him in the line. So, when he completes his task he takes a step up the line, taps the person on the shoulder, and takes over that person's work. That person then does the same, and so on all the way up the line. This simple change can dramatically improve productivity because there is less downtime. Every worker is working all the time. Bucket brigade assembly lines work very well for some companies.

Here is a good example of how an operations team studies processes and makes changes that can have a dramatic impact.

A busy counter clerk at a sandwich shop gets a lot of orders for soft-serve ice cream. The soft-serve machine is kept in the far right corner of the counter. Each time he gets an order for a cone he walks over to the machine and gets one for his customer. The manager of the restaurant observed that the clerk might make literally hundreds of trips to the machine on a busy day. So, the manager installed soft-serve machines in the front center of the counter. Now the counter clerk simply reaches for a cone whenever there is an order. He no longer has to walk so far for each cone. This saves time and enables him to sell many more cones.

Like the bucket brigade example, this example shows how small changes in a process can have a major, direct impact on the company's bottom line. In this example, the restaurant increases the number of ice cream cones that can be sold in an hour by shaving off a few seconds of time for each order. Over the course of a day those seconds add up!

The responsibilities of the operations department depend heavily on the business in which the company is engaged. Product companies might include a manufacturing component. Service companies, on the other hand, don't have manufacturing plants but they might have an elaborate training program to make sure all the employees know how to deliver their service.

Like the marketing department, the operations department often performs a lot of diverse activities. However, unlike in the marketing department, the activities of the operations department are usually more predictable. The assembly line and the counter clerk's work are both examples of predictable behavior.

The key to running a smooth operation is developing the ability to create a repeatable process that can grow as the company grows. It is for this reason that many companies can benefit from hiring low-skilled labor. They can break down processes in ways that make them easy to train people to implement.

One way people in the operations department identify problems is by looking for back-ups or delays in the system. A back-up of unfinished work in one part of the process can cause problems with everything that comes after it, so it's important to understand why work is getting backed up. For instance, an insurance company might have a back-up of unapproved policies. To increase productivity of their staff they might create a process for sorting the applications based on their potential value to the firm. An inexperienced employee can do the sorting, allowing the more experienced—and more expensive - employees to concentrate on the most valuable work before working on lower value applications.

Some of the more common components of the operation include Product Production, Distribution, Supply Chain, Maintenance, Customer Service, Information Technology, and Research & Development. You may recognize these components as also being part of other departments. For instance, Research & Development was also mentioned in our discussion of the Marketing department. Different companies have different organizations. For some companies R&D is a Marketing function and in some companies it is an Operations function. Sometimes it is its own department. It depends on a lot of factors, but ultimately it resides where it is needed most.

Chapter 7

PRODUCT PRODUCTION

Product companies are companies that sell products to customers. In order to do this, they must first acquire the products from suppliers or make the products themselves. Companies that make products must own and operate manufacturing plants. Companies that do not make products must outsource the manufacture of the products to someone else's manufacturing plants.

A manufacturing plant can take many different forms. News stations like to show pictures on television of highly-automated manufacturing plants like automobile factories filled with robotic arms and sophisticated equipment. Large consumer products companies tend to have factories like this. Cars, toasters, TVs, major appliances and large electronics often come from very large automated factories that produce hundreds of thousands of units per year.

The machines you see in big factories include painting robots, automated assembly robots, metal stamping equipment, and large plastic injection molding machines that melt plastic pellets and turn them into plastic parts. Companies invest millions of dollars into this technology and hire highly trained engineers, technicians, mechanics and operators to keep everything running.

These kinds of factories are interesting to watch, but they aren't really a good representation of a typical manufacturing plant. Most plants have lower levels of automation and organization. A small furniture manufacturer, for instance, would look much more like an elaborate wood shop with skilled carpenters working on individual pieces. Most products take a great deal of hands-on work from human beings.

In most factories there is some sort of organized, step-by-step process to make a product from raw materials. Assembly lines are the norm. One person making one product at a time is highly inefficient and is only appropriate for certain art items, custom work, or for very small businesses.

The managers in a manufacturing company are in charge of defining the steps needed to make the product, designing the assembly line, securing the necessary equipment, hiring the right workers, training them to do the job, and making sure they have the supplies they need.

Some factories focus primarily on assembling parts purchased from outside suppliers. An automotive chassis manufacturer, for instance, may not actually make anything. Rather, they order engines, transmissions, axles, brakes, frames and other components from the companies that do make them. They take the completed components and put them together to produce an automotive chassis. Another company will buy the chassis and build the body of the truck on top. The skills needed to build a truck body versus a truck chassis can be quite different so it makes sense to split up these activities.

Some companies take in raw materials from mines and produce completed products. The more steps in the process the company does internally the more vertically integrated it is. Vertical integration refers to how much of the process a company controls. Years ago the phone company would take in raw metal and plastic and produce literally every component of a phone. They would then place the phone in houses and provide phone service. This is a highly vertically integrated example. At the time there weren't many people in the phone-making business so the phone company had to make its own. This kind of vertical integration can be somewhat impractical. Today few phone companies, if any, manufacture their own hardware.

Not all factories make durable products. A winery, for instance, is a factory that crushes grapes and allows them to ferment into wine. It then blends the various wines and bottles it into a final product. In this case most of the work is spent monitoring tanks of wine. The actual crushing grapes part only happens once a year so the needs of the factory change throughout the year.

Likewise, bakeries have processes to turn food ingredients into delicious cakes and cookies. The process includes many different companies. Seed companies sell seeds to farmers. Farmers grow the seeds to grain and sell it to mills. Mills grind the grain into flour and sell it to commercial bakeries. Bakeries bake the flour into baked goods. Along the way there are tractors, trucks, trains, and a multitude of other people helping in the process.

PRODUCT SAFETY

When talking about manufacturing one must also consider a number of safety issues that the operations department has to deal with. There are two primary areas of safety that the operations department worries about. The first is product safety. Product safety includes processes to ensure that food made in a food processing plant is safe to eat, and that products made in a manufacturing company are safe to use. There are lots of government standards that companies must adhere to in order to legally operate in the United States. Even imported products have to adhere to government regulations. Occasionally a product is found to be unsafe, and a company issues a recall. When this happens the company is required by law to repair or replace the product at its own expense for any customer that requests it.

The government has certification programs in safe food handling that employees must participate in before they can handle food. This includes not only food production plants, but also restaurants and bars. Managers in the operations department have to make sure that their employees are trained and certified on an annual basis. Additionally, the physical plant has to be clean and sterile. The government can shut a factory down if it does not adhere to food safety laws. The Food and Drug Administration (FDA) is an extremely powerful government agency.

The other area of safety is worker safety. Factories have a lot of moving equipment, heavy machinery, and repetitive tasks. The Occupational Safety and Health Administration (OSHA) is the government agency that sets and enforces safety standards for US companies. The policies they enforce have been developed based on the vast amount of manufacturing experience of the United States. The US has been manufacturing products in factories since the Industrial Revolution starting in the mid to late 1700's. Before that time most people were farmers or local craftsmen who made products one at a time.

People weren't always concerned with safety. Early factories were very dangerous and workers who were injured rarely received any compensation or assistance. To combat this problem, workers organized themselves into Labor Unions so they could negotiate as a group rather than as individuals. Labor unions are organized around specific trade groups based on their specialized area of expertise. One of the most famous unions is the United Auto Workers (UAW), which represents the interests of workers employed in automotive factories. Today unions concern themselves with safety, wages, insurance, and a number of other related topics. The operations department works closely with the unions to make sure their needs are being met.

Today nearly all countries have a manufacturing component, but not all countries have as much experience as the US. Many of them have only been engaged in serious manufacturing for the past 50 years.

Manufacturing businesses are always under pressure to reduce costs. Because people make up one of the largest costs, managers often look for ways to hire people for less money. In some cases they will build a factory in another country with a lower cost of living. China and Mexico, for instance, are popular places to manufacturer products because workers can be hired at a fraction of what it costs to hire an American or European employee.

Cutting costs sometimes means cutting corners, which can sometimes lead to safety issues. Because most emerging countries don't have as much manufacturing experience as the US, they often have different safety standards. US companies have to be careful when they outsource manufacturing jobs to other countries so that they don't wind up supporting unsafe working environments. American consumers expect that people are treated with the same dignity and respect as American workers.

THROUGHPUT

As long as a factory is considered safe for employees, the operations team can focus some of its attention on throughput. This is the rate at which raw materials become finished products. Like any other business process, the manufacturing process must be carefully monitored, and steps are often changed to improve the speed of manufacture or increase the quality of the product.

In order to sell products, manufacturing companies must take in raw materials and then ship out finished goods. Obtaining raw materials is called Supply Chain Management and shipping out goods is called Distribution. Sometimes people consider Distribution part of Supply Chain Management and vice versa. Like everything you will learn about how businesses work, different companies have their own way of looking at things.

SUPPLY CHAIN

The acquisition of raw materials is part of the supply chain management process. The operations department is responsible for making sure that workers have all the ingredients they need in order to create finished products. This can be a big job for complicated products. In large companies there could be literally thousands of suppliers that supply everything from nuts and bolts to paper towels.

Supply costs can be one of the largest costs a company has, so even small savings on parts can have a dramatic impact on a company's bottom line. Timing of when parts arrive in the factory is important too. It is expensive to store raw materials in a factory so supply chain managers want just enough supplies to get the job done, but not so much they have to store excess supplies. Additionally, they want to order in quantities large enough to get the best price. As you might guess, supply chain managers have to be very analytical and understand the flow of materials into the factory.

DISTRIBUTION

At the other end of the factory, finished products are being picked up by trucks and shipped out to customers. Like supply chain management, distribution managers have to take a lot of different things into account to make sure the flow out of the factory matches the flow into the factory as closely as possible. If products move out more quickly than they come in, the company will run out of products and won't be able to meet demand. If products move out more slowly than they come in, then the company will build up inventory and have to store it—which is expensive. So, distribution managers worry about how much inventory is stored in the warehouse and how full a truck is when it leaves the warehouse. A half-full truck costs the same as a full truck, so the more products they can ship the more money they will save. In many cases they cut deals with other companies to ship their products in the opposite direction. A company in New York might cut a deal with a company in California so that the truck can carry products both directions, again saving time and money.

Distribution managers need to work with production managers so they can plan ahead and get the best pricing. Shipping products on a container ship is much less expensive than shipping on an airplane, but it can take months to get delivery rather than days. Everything is a tradeoff between efficiency and effectiveness, and the operations department makes these kinds of decisions every day.

In B2B companies, the distribution managers ship bulk products to resellers like catalog companies and retailers. In B2C companies, the distribution managers ship individual orders directly to consumers usually through UPS, FedEx, or the postal service.

PICK & PACK

The process of putting products into boxes and preparing them for shipment is known as Pick and Pack. Workers have to have a process of quickly finding products and getting them into the right size box. The easier it is to find products on the shelf, the faster a picker can pack them. To improve the pick and pack process, operations managers might group frequently ordered products together or install a computer system that will tell the pickers where to look on a shelf. Small companies may only have a few items, but large companies could have thousands of products. Pickers at Amazon.com wear roller skates in the warehouse to help them move faster.

The operations team needs to have access to a lot of information in order to do their job. Few product companies can get away without information systems that help them collect, store, access, and analyze data.

INFORMATION TECHNOLGY

Information Technology (IT) is a core function in nearly all businesses. Today just about everyone uses some kind of technology to help run the company. Many companies even have full time Chief Information Officers (CIOs) who report directly to the company President. Information systems are usually part of the operations team. IT managers are responsible for everything from the computers that people work on, to data servers and other equipment connected to the network.

In large manufacturing companies everything is tracked and managed electronically—from the supply chain to the distribution of finished goods. People use tracking numbers, barcodes and other methods for tracking items through the process. The data gets compiled into reports that operations managers can use to identify problems.

Other departments, including finance, accounting, research, and customer service also access information systems.

CUSTOMER SERVICE

Customer Service, in particular, is often tightly linked to the manufacturing process. They help people place orders, and they communicate order status throughout the process. They also help support the products after the sale. You might say that marketing sells the product, but customer service keeps it sold. They keep it sold by supporting it in the field. If a customer can't get a product to perform he might return it in disgust.

If you visit a customer service department you will likely see a room full of cubicles with a lot of people talking into headsets. They use computers to track their interactions, and to access databases with product problem and solution information. They can also track order status and repair status. Most customer service departments have sample rooms that have samples of all the products the company makes. This way workers can look at the products while they help customers solve their problems.

NON-MANUFACTURING OPERATIONS

Of course not every company has a manufacturing plant. Some companies buy products from other companies and sell them directly to consumers or other businesses. Catalog companies, for instance, still have to manage a distribution center and a supply chain. The operational processes are similar, but they don't have to worry about the actual manufacturing process.

Service companies may not have a product focus, but even they have to deal with physical goods. A cable TV company has to keep an inventory of modems, set-top boxes, remote controls, cables, wires and other supplies needed to install and provide in-home entertainment, phone, and internet service. Their inventory may not be as extensive as a product-focused company, but they still deal with supply chain and distribution issues. They also deal with the hiring, training, and management of service providers. This, in itself, is an operational issue that the operations department has to deal with.

JOBS IN OPERATIONS

The most senior manager in the operations department is the Chief Operating Officer. This position is often held by the company President who will have the title President and COO. Below the COO are VP-level positions with a focus on one operational area. For instance a manufacturing company might have a VP of Supply Chain, a VP of Manufacturing and a VP of Distribution. In some cases a company will have a number of separate manufacturing plants or branch offices for service companies. The person who oversees an individual business unit is often called the General Manager. The General Manager acts as a conduit between the COO and lower level staff at certain locations. The VP and General Managers often have advanced degrees in business, engineering, operations, and manufacturing.

Below the Vice Presidents are a variety of Director-level jobs that may be focused on specific areas within the company. The Director of Purchasing, for instance, would be in charge of negotiating prices with suppliers. The Director of Production might be in charge of select assembly operations. Below that are various Line Managers who manage the staff on an assembly line, Parts Managers that make sure the assembly lines have enough parts, and Inventory Specialists who keep track of what is in stock. There are also analysts who compile and interpret reports and many other jobs.

The operations department is the department that ultimately delivers on the company's promise to customers. When they do their job right customers are happy. Happy customers not only stay loyal, they tell other potential customers about their experience. Keeping customers happy is the best way to help a company grow.

Chapter 8

HUMAN RESOURCES

When you were hired, you probably spoke to someone in the Human Resources (HR) Department. HR is the department responsible for making sure that the people working for the company have what they need in terms of training, benefits, and of course, compensation. In most companies HR acts as a support function to make sure that other departments are following proper procedures for hiring. How companies treat their employees is a major concern of the government, and there are many laws that govern our interaction with employees, ranging from minimum wage laws to anti-discrimination laws.

Breaking these laws can have major consequences for employers so they take them seriously.

HIRING

The HR department helps other departments hire people for open positions. Their level of involvement varies depending on the size of the company, but it is not uncommon for HR to assist with everything from posting a job description on a job board, to drafting an offer letter, to negotiating salary and benefits.

SCREENING PROCESS

The hiring process can be cumbersome and time-consuming. These days most job postings get hundreds, if not thousands of responses. Managers have to look through each application to find the best candidates. This is called the screening process and it is not uncommon for a manager to spend a few seconds with an application or a candidate's resume. They are looking for specific experience, skills, and qualifications that pique their interest. In some cases, especially in larger companies, the HR department uses automated software that can read a resume and automatically send a rejection letter if it does not match pre-determined criteria.

Understanding the hiring process can provide some insight to job seekers. For instance, knowing that HR departments receive hundreds or thousands of resumes for a single job opening means that they simply don't have time to give each one a thoughtful review. Most of the time they are looking for clues about an individual that will tell them if he or she is a good fit for the job opening. The clues, however, aren't secrets. They are outlined in the job posting. Therefore, one of the best ways to get a hiring manager's attention is to tweak your resume based on the language used on the job posting. Try to match as many of their job requirements to your experience as possible. If they are asking for graphic designers with experience with Photoshop, and you have that particular skill, make sure that it's clear on your resume and towards the top. Use their words on your resume so you can avoid being overlooked in the screening process. For instance, if the ad is for a day care center and it uses the word *newborns*, be sure to use that word in your resume instead of just the word *babies*. It will help your resume stand out.

In some cases they actually have computer software scan your resume to look for specific words. You can bet the words they are looking for are also in the job posting.

The other place to highlight how your specific skills match the qualifications is to use a cover letter that goes into detail about how you fit their needs based on the job posting. Again, this ensures that when the hiring manager reviews your application, he or she will find what they are looking for. Generic cover letters rarely catch someone's attention. A good cover letter can be one of the most important pieces of your application.

One way to increase your chances of getting through the screening process is to make connections with people who work at the company. You can find people through Facebook, LinkedIn, Twitter, and other social networking sites. You can also try to get access to your college's alumni database. Better yet, attend alumni meetings and industry networking events. These days, face-to-face networking goes a long way in the hiring process. Managers who know you personally can get you an interview.

Most companies allow internal candidates to apply for open positions. Job openings are posted internally for employees to express interest. In these cases, interested candidates prepare and submit their resumes the same as an external candidate would. Before they apply, however, employees should always speak to their supervisor to let them know they are interested in changing jobs. It is considered good business etiquette to keep your manager informed about internal job interviews. Conversely, if you are applying for an external position, it is much more common to keep your search confidential until you actually have an offer on the table.

PHONE SCREEN

The application screening process produces a short list of candidates that the company wants to learn more about. The HR department will usually share the best resumes with the hiring manager. The hiring manager is most often the person who will supervise the employee in the department the employee joins. The hiring manager for a Director of Direct Marketing, for instance, is likely the Vice President of Marketing. The HR department helps the VP as much as possible so he or she can concentrate on running marketing.

The hiring manager and the HR manager discuss which applicants look the most promising. The HR department will reach out to this list to express interest in learning more about the candidates. These days it is quite common to conduct a phone screen before bringing someone in for an in-person interview.

The phone screen isn't an interview, it's a screen. It is designed to weed out undesirable candidates so there will be fewer to interview later. The person calling from HR will probably have a pretty standard set of questions to ask.

They want to know if you have the knowledge, talent and willingness to do the job. Knowledge refers to your understanding and experience with the tasks and processes of a department. If you are interviewing for a corporate counsel position, they will want to know that you have a law degree and a certain level of experience dealing with issues that you are likely to encounter while on the job.

You should understand the requirements of the job so you will be ready to provide the information they need to assess your knowledge. It's always a good idea to have verifiable information. It's one thing to say you have a degree, but you should have the telephone number of the school's registrar so the HR department can verify if they want. They may not ask for this information, but it's nice to have in case they want it. These days companies conduct pre-employment background checks that can include education verification.

Talent refers to your aptitude for the subject matter and how you apply your knowledge. A talented attorney, for instance, is one who learns quickly and is able to apply what he or she learns with consistent results. This requires passion and creativity. Passion means that the subject is not only important to an individual, but also that the individual has a high level of personal identification with the subject. A passionate lawyer is one who identifies himself or herself with the profession of law and the needs of clients. Creativity refers to how you find new ways to approach problems to find new solutions.

You should have some examples about how you creatively solved problems for your clients, or went out of your way to make sure the job was done right. You won't get into depth about your experience during a phone screen, but you will probably be asked to give a little run-down of your career. Be sure to organize your thoughts in advance so you can highlight relevant areas.

Lastly, willingness means that you are inclined to do the job they ask under the terms of employment that they are offering. This means they want to find out your desired salary, whether or not you will travel for work, your ability to relocate if necessary and things like that. They will also ask about your interest in the company's industry and products. If you're applying for a job with a company that makes guns and you are anti-gun then nothing else really matters. If you aren't willing to do the job, the call is over.

Always put your best foot forward during these kinds of calls. Do your research in advance and familiarize yourself with the company and the products so you can speak intelligently to these kinds of questions. Be honest, but always try to keep the tone positive and upbeat. If the HR caller gets a bad feeling about you there isn't much hope.

Not every question is fair game. There are a number of topics that are off limits during an interview to prevent possible discrimination. Interviewers can't legally ask you about your age, race, gender, nationality, religion, disabilities, marital status, or kids. And, while it's not illegal to bring these subjects up yourself, as a job candidate it's best to leave these issues out of the discussion along with your political opinions. These aren't topics that are likely to help your chances of getting a job, and could potentially hurt you. Stick to topics related to the job and your ability to do the job.

The phone screen is not the time to ask about salary, benefits or vacation time. Focus on their needs first. The goal of the phone screen is not to get a job; it's to get an interview. At this point all you can do is lose the opportunity for further consideration.

INTERVIEWS

Candidates who pass the phone screen are invited to interview in person for the position. The HR department will coordinate the visit and schedule the interviews with the right managers and associates. In some cases travel will be required. The HR department will coordinate travel for candidates including airline, car rental, and hotel. In most cases the company will cover these costs. If you travel for an interview, be sure to save your receipts and keep detailed records of expenses.

Interviews typically last about an hour and are one-on-one with managers in the department. Sometimes candidates will have a group interview, but it's not very common. You may have many interviews in one day with different people who have a stake in the decision.

By the time you have arrived at the interview the company has already decided that you are qualified for the job in that you have the knowledge, talent, and willingness to do the job. They will explore these topics in more detail, but the main point of the in-person interview is to assess fit. They want to see if you are the kind of person they want to work with every weekday for years to come. Most people spend more time with their coworkers than they do with their own families.

Students and working professionals are in different peer groups. When you enter the workforce, your peers will become other working professionals. It is important to understand the culture of the peer group you are entering and be careful to demonstrate your compatibility with them.

Everything from how you dress to how you shake hands will be taken into account when they make their final decision. That's why it's so important to dress appropriately, and to be well-rested, upbeat, and prepared for the interview.

One way to leave a positive impression is to do plenty of research on the company and the people who work there — especially those with whom you will be meeting. The HR department can give you a list of names. A little bit of online research will tell you a lot about them. Print out copies of what you find online and bring them to the interview with you in neatly labeled file folders. This will provide tangible evidence of how interested you are in the company and how organized you are. It's a nice touch that will make a great impression. Be sure to send a thank-you note or email to all the people you meet. It's a good idea to recap your value to the firm in your thank-you note so they won't forget who you are.

Depending on the applicant pool and the company's level of interest in certain candidates, the company may want to do several rounds of interviews with the same candidates. When they have picked the person they want to hire, they will make an offer.

OFFERS

The HR department often takes the lead in drafting the offer letter. It usually outlines the basics—title, starting salary, bonus, start date, high-level responsibilities, and a reference to benefits. Sometimes there is a stock option program or commission program as well.

How much a company can pay someone depends on a lot of factors. The HR department keeps on top of competitive salaries for similar companies in their industry. Additionally, larger companies have pre-defined "salary bands" based on department, title, and level of responsibility. This helps them keep payroll costs under control.

The offer letter represents the company's best attempt at attracting you as an employee. Companies usually don't try to "low-ball" potential employees, but they also don't want to overpay someone.

If you receive an offer from a company and it has everything you want, you can accept it as is. However, don't be afraid to negotiate with them if it doesn't have everything you want.

NEGOTIATION

The HR department is often involved in negotiating offers. They usually have some wiggle room with things like base salary and bonus so don't be afraid to ask about reasonable adjustments. In some cases you might have to give up a little in bonus in order to get a larger salary and vice versa. Remember that negotiations are about give and take so be prepared to change your position on things.

Some things are harder to negotiate. Vacation time and health insurance benefits, for instance, may be part of a standard policy for the whole company, so exceptions to the policy would be impractical to manage. If the HR department can't meet your needs they will have to involve the hiring manager.

If the company you are considering has a salary band program that I mentioned before, you might try to negotiate your title in order to get a better compensation package. Make sure the hiring manager understands that you are willing and able to take on greater responsibility in exchange for a higher title. The slight change in title and responsibilities can put you in a salary band with more room for negotiation.

It's much better to look for a job when you are already employed. This gives you time to be selective and gives you more leverage during a negotiation. You can ask for exactly what you want. Worst case scenario is that you are still employed. However, if you are not employed you may feel more desperation. If you are desperate for a job, there is little upside to letting your future employer know about it. Instead, let them know that you are really excited about the job, but that you have a few concerns about the offer, and let them know what you would like. Once an offer has been made, employers are eager to please;   they don't want to move to their second choice or even begin the process over again!

ACCEPTANCE

Once you have accepted an offer there are probably going to be a few more hoops you will need to jump through. The HR department will conduct a background check and possibly a drug screen, which means you will have to go to a drug screening facility before you begin your job. Even small companies do these kinds of checks. They usually wait until after a job offer has been accepted so that they can save money.

The background check provides information about your employment history, criminal convictions, and credit history. Inconsistencies between what you told your future employer and what these reports say are red flags that may lead to a withdrawal of the offer. You don't have to volunteer unflattering information during the interview process, but don't lie if you are asked point-blank about anything. It may help you get an offer, but it won't stick.

STARTING WORK

The HR department is often the first point of contact with a new employee on the first day of work. They will provide an office tour, show you where you will be working, and walk you through the necessary paperwork to get payroll set up as well as any benefits programs you might be entitled to. The paperwork includes forms required by the government such as an I-9, which ensures you can legally work in the US, and a W-2, which is a tax withholding form.

In some cases you may be asked to sign non-disclosure agreements that help protect confidential corporate information and non-compete agreements that will prevent you from working for the company's competitors for a certain length of time. If you are not comfortable signing them you can always tell HR that you would like your attorney to review them first. This may hold up your employment, but they should give you the chance to review the material before you sign. In fact, nearly all the documents you will be presented with can be completed at a later date, but it's easier to sign right away. Be sure to bring several forms of identification with you on your first day.

The HR department keeps all the forms in a file with your name on it. By law you have the right to review your HR file whenever you want, but you may not be able to take copies.

Helping you get all your ducks in a row is known as "onboarding" and it may also include some basic training on your first day. Some companies have extensive training programs. The HR department is usually responsible for these training programs and making sure they are completed. Throughout your employment you may be asked by the HR department to attend training sessions from time to time.

ANNUAL REVIEWS

Another responsibility of the HR department is to manage the annual review process across all departments. A typical annual review is a detailed survey that you will complete and your manager will complete. Usually your assessment of yourself will be similar to your manager's assessment. If not, there may be a significant communication gap. The HR department can help identify these issues and provide ways to reduce potential problems.

Annual reviews are important because they help the company to better understand who is working for them, and to identify areas that may need additional training. In most cases raises and bonuses are tied to your annual review. Employees can expect a small annual increase in salary if they receive a decent assessment as long as the company is doing well and growing. This is called a "cost-of-living" increase and is usually around 1%-2%. Larger increases are only applicable when an employee receives a promotion to a higher level of responsibility, and thus becomes eligible for a higher salary band. You should not expect a raise unless you are making a larger contribution to the company's success.

On an ongoing basis the HR department serves as a resource for the company. They manage payroll, administer benefits programs, provide training, and handle tough personnel problems. Most problems at work should be discussed with your immediate supervisor. However, if your immediate supervisor is the problem, you might be better off discussing the matter with a member of the HR department. They are experienced in handling sensitive matters ranging from a basic clash of personalities to larger issues like sexual harassment and criminal activity.

Wellness programs are increasing in popularity. In an effort to save money on health benefits, many companies are making efforts to keep employees healthier by offering a number of physical and emotional wellness programs. Some even offer contests and incentive programs.

TERMINATION

The last major area of responsibility in the HR department is the proper management of employee termination. How an employee is terminated is just as important as how an employee is hired. Like hiring, there are a number of legal issues that must be managed in order for the company to stay out of trouble.

There are four conditions under which a person can be terminated. First, employees can quit for good reason; second, they can quit for no good reason; third, they can get fired for good reason; and fourth, they can get fired for no good reason.

Each of these reasons has a different set of legal and ethical issues that must be managed. In all cases termination is an emotionally-charged time that must be handled delicately and respectfully. Documentation of the termination process is important because it provides a paper trail which will be necessary if the termination results in any legal action from the employee.

QUITTING FOR GOOD REASON

Quitting a job for good reason implies that certain actions of the company forced you to resign. For instance, if the company moved 100 miles away from your home, you would have a good reason for leaving. Or, if the company adversely changed your responsibilities without a reasonable explanation, you would have a good reason to quit. In cases like this the company should recognize that they are at fault and make the transition out as comfortable as possible, given the resources of the company. They might provide severance payments, unemployment benefits, or outplacement services that can help you find another job. Sometimes companies make decisions that negatively impact hardworking individuals. They should be willing to accept the consequences of their actions by not allowing you to bear the full burden of termination.

QUITTING FOR NO GOOD REASON

Quitting a job for no good reason usually implies that you are leaving for personal reasons. Maybe you accepted another job somewhere else, maybe you don't like your job or the people you work with, or maybe you want to retire. If you don't like your job or the people you work with, it's not the company's fault. It's just bad luck. If the reason isn't the fault of the company then you are quitting with no good reason. You should not expect severance payments, extended health benefits, or any other assistance above and beyond what you are owed under the conditions of your employment.

GETTING FIRED FOR NO GOOD REASON

Just as you can quit for no good reason you can also get fired for no good reason. In a poor economy, companies sometimes have to fire good employees because they can't afford to pay them any longer. This is often referred to as a layoff or a furlough. Mass layoffs are common in bad economies, but a layoff doesn't mean that an employee wasn't effective. When a company lays off employees, they do everything they can to make the transition out of the company as comfortable as possible including severance payments, outplacement services, and extended health benefits.

GETTING FIRED FOR GOOD REASON

The last type of termination is getting fired for good reason. This means that after repeated warnings you simply did not fulfill the requirements of the job, or your behavior was bad enough that people felt threatened by you. Bringing a gun to work, stealing, or sexually harassing a coworker are examples of things that would be grounds for immediate termination for good reason. The company should only pay you what they owe you. You will not be eligible for unemployment benefits and you should not expect any severance payments. Being fired for good reason isn't a good thing and it's hard to get back on track after it happens.

HUMAN RESOURCE JOBS

In small companies, department managers handle their own HR tasks with the help of an administrative support person. However, when a company grows, an HR department becomes a necessity. The senior HR managers often have advanced degrees in business with specialization in Human Resources or counseling. Other HR jobs include benefits administrators, recruiters, training managers, and even attorneys who deal with employee issues. HR is a good place for you if you like dealing with people and are well-organized.

HR is an essential function in most businesses and it is a department that touches every person in a company.

Chapter 9

FINANCE & ACCOUNTING

Few areas within a business are as misunderstood as finance and accounting. This is because their skill sets are closely related and they both deal with the company's money. However, their functions are quite different. The simplest explanation is that the role of the Accounting Department is to tell a company *what has happened*, financially, in the business, and the role of Finance is to advise the company *what to do next*.

Let's say you want to figure out your personal finances. First you would sit down and create a list of all things related to your money. You might start with how much money you have in your checking and savings accounts and in any investment accounts you might own. Next you count up all your outstanding debt, such as car loans, credit card balances or student loans. After that you could make a list of all your expenses—rent, food, gas, loan payments—and income—money from a job, gifts you might get from your parents, etcetera. Once you have all of this information, you might want to create a budget by extrapolating out a few months to see what your financial situation might be in a few months or a year. The process of gathering all this information and organizing it so it can be understood is accounting.

Let's say you want to buy a new car. In order to figure out how to pay for the car you would want to assess how much you can afford, based on the notes you prepared when you were accounting for everything. You would have to research what kind of car you want, decide how much of a down payment you could afford to pay, and then figure out how to cover the rest. You could apply for a car loan, put the balance on a credit card or even talk with your parents. The process of figuring out how you are going to pay for the car while still maintaining your current lifestyle is finance.

Accounting tells you where you have been and where you are currently. Finance helps you decide what to do in the future. In many ways accounting is a subset of Finance, but that does not diminish its importance. Many corporate CEOs have accounting backgrounds. To understand accounting is to understand the value of a good business model.

The Chief Financial Officer usually has direct responsibility for the finance and accounting functions of a business. One of his or her main functions is to provide the President and CEO with financial reports that outline the financial situation of the company—good or bad. The CFO does this by preparing financial statements.

FINANCIAL STATEMENTS

There are three types of financial statements. A Balance Sheet, Income Statement, and Cash Flow Statement. These three documents are used in most companies to provide information about a company's financial heath at any point in time.

BALANCE SHEET

A Balance Sheet is called a balance sheet because it balances the company's assets against its liabilities and owner's equity. Assets refer to company property, tangible and intangible. Cash, inventory, equipment and land are examples of assets. Liabilities refer to money owed to someone else, including outstanding loans, and bills that need to be paid. When you subtract your liabilities from your assets you have the portion of the assets that are outright owned by the owners of the company. This is known as owner's equity or stockholder's equity. In order to be balanced, Assets must equal Liabilities plus Owner's Equity, often expressed as $A = L + OE$.

The Balance Sheet gives investors a sense of how well their investment has been deployed and how likely they are to get a return on investment. For instance, if the company's liabilities are so high that owner's equity is small, investors may worry that the company won't be able to pay its bills on time. Conversely, if the liabilities are small, the investors might want to know why the company doesn't borrow more money to accelerate growth.

For nonprofit organizations the Balance Sheet is a little different because nonprofit organizations don't have owners. So, instead of owner's equity, nonprofits use the term Net Assets to imply what is left over after liabilities have been subtracted. It's the same concept, but reflects the fact that there are no owners. Additionally, nonprofit organizations prefer to use the term Statement of Financial Position, rather than Balance Sheet, for this particular report.

It might seem like a financial statement would be pretty cut and dry. After all, your bank balances are what they are. However, managers make a lot of decisions that impact how their financial statements look. For instance, Balance Sheets for manufacturing companies list the value of their inventory under assets. The value is recorded at the cost of the inventory. When the inventory is sold, the value of the inventory is deducted from the total. However, the cost of inventory can fluctuate, sometimes quite dramatically. So, sometimes the cost of the inventory is higher than at other times, but the inventory is all mixed together so it's hard to figure out which products cost more and which products cost less. Managers have to decide which cost they will deduct. They need to be not only honest in their reporting, but also they need to make sure their financials communicate the right message.

FIFO and LIFO

Consider the cost of a product made from plastic. Plastic is a petroleum-based material. So, the price of plastic pellets used in the manufacturing process changes based on the price of oil. Therefore, the cost of the inventory of products made from plastic changes nearly every time the company replenishes inventory. In order to report this accurately, the company needs to make a decision. They might choose a method called Last In First Out (LIFO), by which they would deduct the cost of the *most recent inventory* from the Balance Sheet. Or, they might choose the opposite approach called First In First Out (FIFO), by which they would deduct the cost of the *oldest inventory* from the Balance Sheet. The method they use can have a large impact on the Balance Sheet. Most companies have a list of notes that accompanies their Balance Sheet which explains these kinds of decisions.

Your personal Balance Sheet would include personal assets, such as the cash in your checking and savings accounts, and the value of any major assets you owned, such as a house or a car. Personal liabilities would include student loans, car loans, credit cards, and money you owed to utilities or landlords, and other obligations. Whatever is left over is your "owner's equity" which is more commonly known as your net worth.

Balance Sheet

2014
(all numbers in $000)

ASSETS		LIABILITIES	
Current Assets		Current Liabilities	
Cash		Accounts payable	
Accounts receivable		Short-term notes	
(less doubtful accounts)		Current portion of long-term notes	
Inventory		Interest payable	
Temporary investment		Taxes payable	
Prepaid expenses		Accrued payroll	
Total Current Assets		Total Current Liabilities	
Fixed Assets		Long-term Liabilities	
Long-term investments		Mortgage	
Land		Other long-term liabilities	
Buildings		Total Long-Term Liabilities	
(less accumulated depreciation)			
Plant and equipment			
(less accumulated depreciation)		Shareholders' Equity	
Furniture and fixtures		Capital stock	
(less accumulated depreciation)		Retained earnings	
Total Net Fixed Assets		Total Shareholders' Equity	
TOTAL ASSETS		TOTAL LIABILITIES & EQUITY	

INCOME STATEMENT

The second type of financial statement is called an Income Statement. It shows money coming in and money going out. The Balance Sheet will have a line for income, but the Income Statement will explain why income is what it is. Most people like the Income Statement because it shows the company's profit. In fact, the document is sometimes called the Profit & Loss Statement. On it you will see all the sources of income. The main source of income is sales of products or services. This is known as Revenue. Other sources of income could be interest income, royalties, or rent. There are many options, but most of the time money from customers is reported as revenue.

Your personal sources of income could be your salary, income from investments, or even money from your parents if they still help you out. Money given to you that you have to pay back isn't income because it's not really yours.

Nonprofit organizations don't have Income Statements because that would imply a profit motive that does not exist in the nonprofit world. However, similar information is captured on a Statement of Activities. In a nonprofit organization revenue refers to donations, grants, and money raised through other activities like fundraisers.

Most companies have a few different revenue streams but the smaller the company is, the fewer they will have. From the revenue we subtract all of the various expenses that we incur in order to earn the revenue.

There are two primary "buckets" of expenses. Variable expenses are those that change based on the number of products sold or services provided. If you sell bananas, for instance, the cost of the bananas is variable because it changes based on how many bananas you sell. Likewise, if you sell pest control services, the cost of the supplies used in the house-call are variable.

Fixed costs, on the other hand, are not directly dependent on the number of products sold. Rent, for instance, would be the same regardless of the volume of products. Of course you might need a bigger warehouse if your company sold so many products it ran out of room, but a fixed expense isn't as fluid as a variable expense. However, because there is a grey area, managers need to make decisions about how to report expenses on the Income Statement.

In many cases product companies deduct the variable costs from Revenue under a category called Cost of Goods Sold (COGS). This way, readers of the Income Statement can see exactly how much they have to work with to operate the company. With COGS deducted from Revenue you get the difference, which is known as Gross Revenue. This is the amount of money the company has to operate the business. Whatever is left over is available for taxes and profits.

Cost of Goods Sold includes product costs as well as transportation costs associated with getting the materials to the factory and getting the finished goods out to customers.

The next section on the Income Statement is the expenses section. This includes every expense in the company including rent, salaries, office furniture, electricity, computers, heat, office supplies, health insurance, travel expenses, and anything else the company needs to run the company. These are generally known as Operating Expenses because they relate to the operations of the company. If you think back to the earlier discussion of Operations you may remember that Operations determines the profits of the company. When you look at the Income Statement it's easy to see why: the vast majority of expenses in a company are operating expenses.

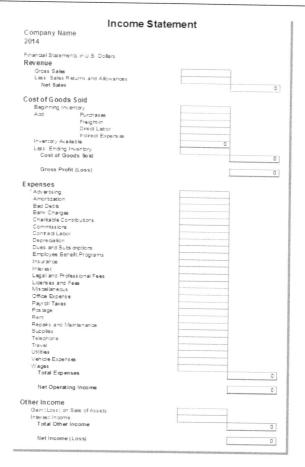

CASH FLOW STATEMENT

The last major financial statement for a company is the Cash Flow Statement. This document reports on the movement of cash into and out of a company. In some ways the Cash Flow Statement is similar to the Income Statement. However, the Cash Flow Statement takes into account the timing of payments so managers can see exactly when cash is coming in or going out. Each month, for example, the company gets a phone bill. The phone bill is included on the Income Statement as an expense. However, the company may not actually pay the phone bill right away. So, even though the company incurred an expense, no actual cash exchanged hands. If the company pays the bill the following month it will be recorded on the Cash Flow Statement the following month. Similarly, a company may make a sale and deliver goods to a customer. The sale is recorded on the Income Statement under revenue. However, the company may not have received a payment from the customer. The customer may have negotiated special payment terms allowing them an extra thirty days to pay the bill. In this case the cash wouldn't be received for another thirty days after the company sent the invoice.

The Balance Sheet will tell managers how much cash they have on hand, the Cash Flow Statement lets managers know why the cash balance is what it is. Both for-profit companies and nonprofit organizations use a Cash Flow Statement. No matter what kind of business environment you are in, cash is always a top concern!

Statement of Cash Flows

Cash flows from operating activities
Cash received from customers
Cash paid for merchandise
Cash paid for wages and other operating expenses
Cash paid for interest
Cash paid for taxes
Other
Net cash provided (used) by operating activities

Cash flows from investing activities
Cash received from sale of capital assets (plant and equipment, etc.)
Cash received from disposition of business segments
Cash received from collection of notes receivable
Cash paid for purchase of capital assets
Cash paid to acquire businesses
Other
Net cash provided (used) by investing activities

Cash flows from financing activities
Cash received from issuing stock
Cash received from long-term borrowings
Cash paid to repurchase stock
Cash paid to retire long-term debt
Cash paid for dividends
Other
Net cash provided (used) in financing activities
Increase (decrease) in cash during the period
Cash balance at the beginning of the period
Cash balance at the end of the period

The three main financial statements —the Balance Sheet, Income Statement and Cash Flow Statement—are important tools that managers need to understand the health of their company. The Chief Financial Officer is responsible for making sure these reports are prepared on a regular basis and whenever other managers need them.

The data on the financial statements is collected by the company's accounting system. Employees enter this information every time a financial event takes place. A financial event could be income, expenses, payments, or receipts. There are two main departments within the Accounting Department that manage these efforts. Accounts Payable and Accounts Receivable.   In smaller companies, these two groups may be consolidated into one. Large companies may have dozens of people in each group.

ACCOUNTS PAYABLE

The accounts payable team has two main functions. The first is to record expenses as they are incurred; the second is to make payments. In most cases the company will want to hold onto its cash as long as possible. When they get a bill or invoice from a vendor they will record it in their accounting software, and set a reminder to pay the bill when it is due. The company will negotiate credit terms with suppliers that allow them to wait a certain amount of time after receiving a bill before they have to pay it. Thirty days is a typical timeframe. You, too, have credit terms with people. Your credit card bill probably doesn't have to be paid on the day you receive it. You probably have at least a month before the payment is due.

ACCOUNTS RECEIVEABLE

Like the Accounts Payable team, the Accounts Receivable team has two main functions. The first is to record revenue as it is earned; the second is to collect the money. When the sales team makes a sale, they alert Accounts Receivable. The Accounts Receivable team creates and invoice and sends it to the customer. When the invoice is sent, the company "books" the revenue, meaning they count the invoice as Revenue on the Income Statement. Next, the Accounts Receivable team monitors the payment due dates on the invoices it sends, and starts reaching out to customers who have not paid on time. This is known as collections. When the payment is made, the Accounts Receivable team records the payment and the cash is reported on the Cash Flow Statement.

Besides recording revenue and collecting money, the Accounts Receivable team is usually the department that provides credit terms to customers. Companies give certain customers extended payment terms to make it easier to pay. Customers who don't have credit terms have to either pay in advance or provide cash on delivery of products, also known as "C.O.D." If a customer prefers to pay after receiving the product or service—also known as "terms" – the customer can submit a credit application. The credit application is a form that requests information about the customer, the number of years in business (if the customer is a company), the customer's history of paying debts in a timely manner, and even personal references. The Accounts Receivable team will review the application and assess the risk of the customer not paying. If the risk is low they will provide payment terms and usually a credit limit for how much the customer can order before having to pay off some or all of the account.

Like all departments, the Accounting team has its own processes for managing its work. The Accounts Payable team has a process for processing an invoice from a vendor, a process for tracking the consumption of materials in a factory, a process for tracking taxes, a process for payroll, and a process for making sure that employees get reimbursed for expenses they incur on behalf of the company. Many of these processes touch other employees in the company.

In most companies, the Accounting Department serves as a support function or a back-office function. This means they aren't usually the people in front of customers, or making spending decisions. Therefore, they need input from people who are. When an Accounting Department process touches employees in other departments it's usually because they need to know where the money is coming from or going to.

One of the most common interactions between employees and the Accounting Department has to do with expense reporting. When you incur costs on behalf of the company, you can expect to be reimbursed. For instance, you might go on a business trip. Most of your travel expenses will be covered by the company, but you need to pay them first out of your own pocket. When you get back from the trip you will need to complete an expense report. The main point of the expense report is to let the Accounting Department know how to categorize your spending. This way the expenses can be put under the right line items on the financial statements and other reports. In most cases your expense report will have to be approved by your manager. This check ensures that the report is accurate and that you had the authority to incur costs on behalf of the company.

When invoices and bills are received, the Accounting Department routes them to the manager that authorized the purchase. The manger will write an account number on the invoice as part of the approval for it to be paid. Again, this tells the Accounting Department how to categorize the expense. It also helps ensure that only legitimate invoices are being paid.

The processes in the Accounting Department tend to be stricter than those in other departments. Forms need to be completed, the right signatures need to be captured, and the numbers need to be right so that the department can create the right reports.

Getting the right reports is important because the Finance Department has to deal with the Internal Revenue Service (IRS) to pay taxes. How money is categorized sometimes determines whether or not it can be taxed. For instance, money spent *on travel* can usually be deducted from taxable income, but only a fraction of money spent *on meals* can be deducted from taxable income. Mistakes can cost the company extra taxes, or it can lead to underpayment of taxes—which can get the company in real trouble with the IRS if they are ever audited.

The IRS isn't the only entity that legally requires accurate reporting. The Securities Exchange Commission (SEC) monitors publicly-traded companies and requires that all financial statements be audited by a third-party accounting firm.

Banks require accurate reporting for bank loans and lines of credit. If the bank finds an error in a financial statement it could change its mind about loaning the company money. It could even call loans already in place (requiring early payment), thereby forcing the company to pay the bank back immediately.

In addition to processing money and creating reports, the Finance Department and the Accounting Department help the company with financial planning.

BUDGETING

The annual budgeting process is often managed by the Finance Department, in close cooperation with the Accounting Department. During the budgeting process, managers throughout the company are asked to forecast what they expect their spending needs will be. Budgets are a projection of what the company hopes will happen in the next year or so.

In established companies, the budgeting process usually builds on what happened the year before. In newer companies with less of a track record, projections need to be created based on a variety of assumptions about the market, and on what they will need to serve customers.

Individual managers submit their team's budget and the Finance Department will consolidate them to create an overall budget projection which includes both revenue and expenses. Using this information they can build future-facing financial statements to use as planning tools.

Creating the overall corporate budget is a very big job. Once it is complete the people in the Finance Department go to work figuring out how to make sure they have enough money to support the budget. In some cases they might have to borrow money to cover expenses, depending on when they plan on getting paid. A company that makes Christmas decorations, for instance, might have to take out a loan to cover costs until it is able to start collecting money from customers at Christmastime.

The annual budget and financing plan must be approved by the senior management team and the Board of Directors, if the company has one.

The approved budget is an important document in most companies. It outlines what a team or department is authorized to spend and it helps set the company's goals, which are often the basis for bonus and commission programs.

Finance and Accounting are closely related. Remember that Accounting's focus is on tracking, categorizing, and managing the money coming into and out of a company. The job of finance is to make sure the company has the money it needs to run.

Chapter 10

THE BUSINESS LIFECYCLE

Throughout this book we have tried to highlight the core functions of a business using broad terms and some important generalizations. In your own life you will encounter companies that may approach the activities within each function differently. However, you will never find a business that doesn't do at least some kind of accounting, marketing, sales, operations, human resources, and basic management functions. The size and scope may vary, but without certain functions the business simply isn't a business. For instance, there is no such thing as a business that doesn't generate revenue sooner or later. If there is no revenue there is no business. A business without revenue is a hobby. In fact, the IRS will legally treat your business as a hobby for tax purposes.

All companies have a lifecycle with a beginning and an ending. Some companies last a long time. Kongo Gumi, a company in Japan that builds temples was in business over 1,400 years before it was acquired by another company in 2006. Most companies, however, don't last very long. In fact, the majority of new companies go out of business within a few years. Their ability to stay in business will depend upon their ability to not only create something of value for customers that can be delivered for less than it costs the company, but also to develop the right business processes so that their business can grow.

Getting your bearings in your company and understanding how it works has a lot to do with understanding its stage in development.

STARTUP COMPANIES

Each year literally millions of entrepreneurs start companies all over the world. Over 500,000 start in the United States alone. In a start-up company all the functions are handled by a few people. A solo entrepreneur is every department at once. There may not be much of a Human Resource function for a one-person operation, but the function still exists. Entrepreneurs must pay themselves (if they can), secure their own insurance, and do other Human Resource-related activities even if only on a small scale.

IDEA STAGE

The first step in starting a company is to establish the basic idea, and to assemble the appropriate foundation upon which the company will be built. This is the *idea stage*, and most of the activity is talking, planning, and outlining the initial strategy. This stage often takes place in homes, coffee shops, and other informal places. There isn't much thought put into structure because everyone is trying to figure out what needs to be done and how to do it. Even solo entrepreneurs talk to friends, family colleagues, potential customers, and potential partners. There is a lot of talk at the idea stage, but probably not a lot of action. Some people talk for years about their ideas before doing anything. Hopefully, if the talk is exciting enough, the people will begin putting the ideas into action and start figuring out if their concept is viable.

Nonprofit organizations often start with a group of like-minded individuals simply volunteering their time to solve a problem for someone in need. If their solution works, the group may want to bring it to other people in need.

The need will determine the demand for the solution, and the organization's ability to find volunteers or raise money to provide the solution will determine how well they are able to meet the demand.

For-profit companies aren't much different, but the company's motivation is more about its ability to generate profitable income for the founders and investors.

PROOF OF CONCEPT

The first operational stage of a company or organization is Proof of Concept. This is the stage where things move from talk to action. The founding team builds basic versions of its product or service and starts to figure out what customers want to buy. We have discussed the importance of process throughout this book. This is true for start-up companies too. In a start-up company the main task is to invent processes. In more established companies the main task is to refine existing processes.

Every company needs to build business processes that will allow them to grow. Nobody can make a decent living doing random, one-off tasks. A company needs to develop an offering and a way to promote that offering to the outside world. Early business processes focus on this effort by building and testing products in front of customer prospects. The process may not be written or formalized but the company is creating a process by trial and error. When they find a process that works they will invest in it to grow the company. For instance, if they find that the process of placing online ads is a good way to get new customers they will invest in online ads.

Even early-stage startups will divide and conquer as they add people. The solo entrepreneur will find partners or employees that complement his or her own strengths. A strong marketing entrepreneur might hire or partner with someone with a good operations background. Even the smallest companies need to organize themselves in order to succeed.

Sooner or later, the process will stop working properly and will need to be refined, or a new process will need to be created. The President of a startup may create a process for searching the internet for employee prospects and emailing them personally. This process might work for a few new people here and there, but if the company wants to hire dozens of people the President will become overwhelmed and will need a new process. He or she may even have to hire a person who will be dedicated to hiring people. The new process for a few dozen hires may not work when the company has to hire hundreds. This process of creating new and better processes is how a company grows. When a process allows a company to grow inexpensively it is called a *scalable* process. Start-up companies are always looking for processes that scale.

Start-up companies are very fluid places to work. They are in a constant state of flux as they try to build a business model that can grow. As they grow they will hire people to concentrate on areas that need attention, as was described in the hiring example. However, just when one bottleneck is fixed, another may crop up. Entrepreneurs do their best to plan ahead, but with no historical track record for the company, it is difficult to predict what will happen next.

During the Proof-of-Concept stage the company founders will figure out if their idea can actually make money, and if they can create an organization that will turn into a money-making machine. In the case of nonprofit organizations, they will figure out if there is a need for what they want to provide. This requires creating something predictable in an unpredictable environment.

If they have done things properly they will be able to show potential investors that they have a predictable way of generating income. If the investors believe in the start-up concept and team, they will invest in the startup. In the case of a nonprofit, the donors must believe that the organization can help people in need for a reasonable cost.

GROWTH

Once a company has proven that the concept has the ability to become a business, the company will accept outside investment, if it needs it, and focus on growth. This is an exciting time for start-up companies as they build their business beyond the founding team into a real company.

Start-up companies get their reputation of being fast-based, energetic places to work because of the growth phase. Everything is new — new offices, new furniture and equipment, and new people. Not all companies get to this phase. Many companies fail to create a concept for a product or service that anyone actually wants. Or, they may create something people want, but they can't cover the cost of delivering the product or service with the revenue they generate.

During the growth phase companies are busy creating and refining processes to allow them to grow more quickly. The processes they design become more specialized and formal. It is during this time that a formal departmental organization begins to develop.

Accounting is one of the first areas where formal structure and process is needed. Like large companies, start-up companies have to pay taxes so they will need accurate reporting tools to keep organized. Even solo entrepreneurs need a way of keeping track of expenses. Small companies invest in accounting software to help them, and sometimes work with external accountants. This allows them to implement the structure without taking on full-time employees.

Next, production processes begin to get more formalized as companies need to produce products or deliver services according to what the sales team has promised to the customer. Quality control becomes a big issue with rapidly growing firms because they lack a formalized process with the right checks and balances. It's okay though— mistakes happen and it's all about how the company learns and grows. Most new products or services have a few rough edges. Only established companies with millions to invest can wait for a product or service to be "perfect" before they launch it.

The cash requirements of growing companies often outpace their ability to collect cash from paying customers. Therefore, many growing companies spend a lot of time speaking with banks—for loans—or investors—for cash investments in exchange for ownership in the company. When this happens there is a need for a formalized financing function in the company led by the CFO who can manage these efforts on behalf of the firm.

If the company is successful in building a business model that allows them to grow profitably and successfully, they have a lot of financing options because many people will want to be part of the action. Investors will put up the cash because they are confident that they will get a good return and banks will loan money.

In nonprofit organizations, a company will grow rapidly if their positive impact is clear. Donors who want their money to go to a good cause will see the results and want to be part of the positive influence the organization has on a community.

When a company goes to private investors or banks to raise money, they will not only give up ownership in the company, but also some control. The investors and lenders will exert influence and control over how the money is spent, and how the company is run, by joining the company's Board of Directors. The entrepreneur can no longer make unilateral decisions. He or she must run decisions by the board for permission and oversight. As you might remember from earlier, the members of the board represent the interests of the investors.

In a nonprofit organization the donors will also want a Board of Directors. In nonprofits the Board of Directors represents the interests of the general public, to make sure the organization is making the most good from the money it receives.

INITIAL PUBLIC OFFERING

In some cases a company will want so much money to fund growth that private banks and institutions simply can't provide enough cash. An initial public offering (IPO) is a financing option that raises money from people like you and me. In an IPO, the company offers shares in its company through a stock exchange like the New York Stock Exchange or the NASDAQ Stock Market. Through these exchanges individuals can purchase shares of the company stock through authorized brokers and traders. IPOs not only enable the company to raise large amounts of cash, but early investors can later sell their shares and take home lots of money.

As lucrative as an IPO can be, a publicly-traded company has to meet a lot of legal requirements and make regular financial and other legal disclosures to the general public. In public companies, the Chief Financial Officer has to hire a lot of expensive third-party auditors and send out lots of announcements and notices to potentially thousands of shareholders. In public companies the shareholders elect the members of the Board of Directors.

In a growth company investors invest because they think the company will continue to grow, and they can later sell their ownership in the company for more money than they paid for it.

DIVERSIFICATION

All companies go through good times and bad times. In nearly all cases a company's growth will slow down or plateau. This may be because they have penetrated the market with their product or service, or because their internal processes and resources aren't able to continue to produce at the same rate. Plateauing is a natural part of a business life cycle. When a company is facing a plateau they need to find ways of getting over the plateau to continue growing. Diversification is the stage, after growth, when the company introduces new products, or enters new markets in hopes of finding ways to continue generating more revenue. A company that sells lemonade, for instance, might diversify by selling snacks to go with the lemonade. Most medium and large companies have more than one product offering. This is because the company has been around for a while and has plateaued with just the initial product or service offering. Start-up companies don't have the time or the money to focus on many products or services at once. They must focus attention on products with the highest potential first, and build the processes needed to deliver them. Once the processes and systems are in place it's easier to diversify.

Sometimes a company can diversify and enter a new growth stage. Apple computer, for instance, developed the iPod after being in the personal computer business. The iPod brought them into a new stage of high growth. When iPod sales began to plateau they introduced the iPhone to enter a new growth stage. When the iPhone plateaued they introduced the iPad. Of course, at the same time they are upgrading their iPods and iPhones and iPads while they work on the next big thing. They may find it and enter a new round of growth, or they may not find it and continue to diversify by creating different versions of their existing products.

There are a lot of companies at this stage. They don't move as fast or change as much, but they could still be good places to work, and be profitable for investors. Companies in this stage are likely to have more clear-cut functions than smaller companies. The departments and jobs we have discussed in this book are all operating at this stage.

When people invest in companies at the diversification stage they are not necessarily expecting to later sell their ownership at a profit. Rather, they are looking for dividend payment and slower growth. Because companies at the diversification stage have built predictable processes they have more predictable outcomes, and the investment carries less risk. A less risky investment means money is safer; it also means smaller returns.

HARVEST/EXIT

When a company is successfully diversified it becomes more stable and predictable. It may plod along for years in this state with little interest in change or growth. The investors are happy with their predictable returns, and everything is just fine.

However, sooner or later the owners of the company will want to move on. Maybe they thirst for the start-up life, maybe they are older and want to retire, or maybe they don't feel as confident as they used to about the market. Whatever the reason, they may want to sell the company and move onto the next thing. This is called a Harvest phase—when the company stops investing in new products and services, and reduces costs in other areas, with the goal of maximizing whatever future profits they can. They will run on old equipment, stop investing in marketing, and otherwise harvest the value created by the firm. They could even put the company up for sale.

You are unlikely to get a new job with a company at this stage because they generally don't hire many people!

When other people see this happening they may think that they can do a better job than the current management team. They may meet with the owners of the company to discuss a merger or sale. If the price is right, the owners will exit the company by selling it to someone else who wants to be in that market.

In other cases, the company's attempts to diversify are not successful and the market for their product or service offering has waned. Managers who built the large organization can no longer support the costs of running the organization. In order to avoid bankruptcy they may solicit potential buyers. In some cases they will liquidate the company's assets and close the doors.

When one company is acquired by another company, the buying company will usually investigate the company to be acquired very thoroughly. They will keep the parts of the company that are running well and making money, and they will get rid of the parts of the company that aren't working well or are redundant. Most companies don't need more than one accounting department, for instance.

Many people find this final stage of a company's life sad. However, it falls within the natural course of business and it happens all the time. It may cause a career setback for some, but it's an opportunity to try something new at the same time. Even Kongo Gumi, the 1,400 year-old company mentioned earlier, exited the world by getting acquired by another company.

The business lifecycle, is a natural process that all companies go through. They start with an idea, they prove their concept, they grow, they diversify, and they end through a harvest or exit. The time between beginning and end varies dramatically, but the stages are pretty clear.

Chapter 11

CONCLUSION

Understanding how a business works means understanding that businesses are simply a set of processes and systems that allow people to produce something of value. Similar processes are grouped into departments where people who specialize in particular areas can improve the processes over time.

In for-profit companies the processes serve to provide a profitable return on investment for the company's investors. In nonprofit organizations the processes serve to provide benefits to those who need them.

Business processes are designed to increase the efficiency and effectiveness of the business. In some cases a company can improve both, but it other cases there is a tradeoff. The company's managers make decisions based on their assessment of the potential risks and benefits of those tradeoffs. The more risk a decision carries, the more power will be required to make the decision. Higher-level managers have the power to make risky decisions, with the Board of Directors having the final say.

Your job function at a company or organization will be part of one or more of the company's processes. It is your job to understand how the process works, why it exists, and how it is done. The better you become at executing a process the better you will perform. When you understand the processes well enough you will begin to see areas for improvement. You eventually will be able to design your own processes to improve the delivery of products and services. When you become good at not only executing processes, but also designing new ones, you will begin to get promoted through the ranks of the company or organization.

All companies are different, but all companies have certain building blocks that enable them to survive. Understanding the basics is your first step to a successful career in business.

Thank you for taking the time to learn about Business Basics. We hope that the lessons in this program have helped you better understand how you can best fit in your own role, and have taught you how business works.

ABOUT THE AUTHORS

Mike Moyer has spent his career writing, teaching and working in business. His experience includes a wide variety of industries including insurance industry clients, education, technology, consumer goods and even fine wine.

Mike has a MS in Integrated Marketing Communication from Northwestern University and an MBA from the University of Chicago. He teaches business and management at both universities covering topics ranging from marketing, sales, finance, operations and career strategy.

Mike is also the author of *How to Make Colleges Want You, Slicing Pie, Pitch Ninja, Trade Show Samurai* and *Perfect Parent Hats.*

Jerry Fuller is the Executive Director of the James S. Kemper Foundation, an organization dedicated to developing well-rounded future business leaders with a special focus on the insurance industry.

Prior to joining the Kemper Foundation, Jerry was the Executive Director of the Associated Colleges of Illinois (ACI), a network of four year, non-profit, private colleges and universities. Under Jerry's leadership, the ACI became one of the most successful higher education associations in the nation, winning an unprecedented four Distinguished Performance Awards from the Foundation for Independent Higher Education, the George W. Foreman Innovation Award, and Awards of Excellence from the Workforce Board of Metropolitan Chicago and the National College Access Network.

Jerry is a graduate of Northwestern University, received his MBA from The University of Chicago, and completed the Strategic Perspectives in Nonprofit Management Program at the Harvard Business School.

Business Basics Online Course

The online Business Basics course is available at www.JSKemper.org.

www.ingramcontent.com/pod-product-compliance
Lightning Source LLC
LaVergne TN
LVHW050157030125
800442LV00011B/211